Far Away and Long Ago

YOUNG HISTORIANS IN THE CLASSROOM

Monica Edinger

Stephanie Fins

Stenhouse Publishers
York, Maine

Stenhouse Publishers, 431 York Street, York, Maine 03909

www.stenhouse.com

Library of Congress Cataloging-in-Publication Data
Edinger, Monica, 1952-
    Far away and long ago : young historians in the classroom / Monica
Edinger, Stephanie Fins.
        p.   cm.
    Includes bibliographical references (p.) and index.
    ISBN 1-57110-044-X (alk. paper)
    1. History—Study and teaching (Elementary)—New York (State)—
New York—Case studies.   2. Project method in teaching—New York
(State)—New York—Case studies.   3. Interdisciplinary approach in
education—New York (State)—New York—Case studies.   4. Dalton
School (New York, N.Y.) I. Fins, Stephanie, 1950-   . II. Title.
LB1582.U6E35 1997
372.89'09747'1—dc21   97-25727
                                                              CIP

Cover images are from two different projects: the Pilgrim project and
the Northwest Coast project
Cover and interior design by Joyce C. Weston
Cover photograph by Julia Stokien
Chapter opener photographs by Barbara Julius and Stephanie Fins
Typeset by Octal Publishing

Manufactured in the United States of America on acid-free paper
02 01 00 99 98 97 9 8 7 6 5 4 3 2 1

Contents

Preface

History begins as stories. Ours starts in New York City, where we both live and work. A crowded, intense place, New York can often seem like the center of the universe to its inhabitants, but far away and irrelevant to everyone else. It is challenging to help urban children gain a sense of life's diversity beyond the city limits. Seasoned New Yorkers now, both of us have lived and worked far from the island of Manhattan: Stephanie, an anthropologist at the American Museum of Natural History, has done field work in Peru; Monica, a fourth-grade teacher at the Dalton School, is a former Peace Corps volunteer in Sierra Leone.

Our personal and professional camaraderie is of long standing. It began in the classroom as we worked together creating curriculum and teaching Monica's students. It moved beyond the school as our intellectual connection developed. Both of us are lifelong learners, always exchanging new ideas. You can often find us together at bookstores buying more books than either of us can afford or at our local Starbucks conversing animatedly over lattes. We live within a few blocks of each other and have been known to stand on the sidewalk chatting for far too long about a successful classroom activity or with equal enthusiasm about a new neighborhood restaurant. We have supported each other through personal crises and family illnesses. The history we share is important to both of us, and the stories of our personal lives blend into those of our professional lives, making us passionate teachers and learners.

This book began as a conversation. We had been creating social studies curriculum together for some years when circumstances caused us to become more interested specifically in history. Parents at Monica's school were demanding a greater emphasis on history; the National History Standards had recently come out, and the subject of teaching history was becoming more prominent in the media. As we talked about the place of history in a social studies curriculum, about how to teach and learn history, about what history meant to us, the ideas at the heart of this book began to emerge.

The setting is Monica's fourth-grade classroom, primarily during the 1995–96 and 1996–97 school years. Our aim is to show a teacher learning what it means to teach history and children learning how to do history. In the first chapter Monica presents her ideas about learning and teaching history; in subsequent chapters she focuses on specific units that illustrate different aspects of teaching history. These chapters move from personal history to distant history; however, this is not to suggest that personal history must come before other kinds of history. We see no reason why a first grader can't become deeply engaged in a study of ancient Greece with the help of a passionate teacher, or why an eighth grader can't be inspired to write a personal memoir. One kind of history does not need to be taught before the other. Similarly, what is far away and long ago can be different things to different people. Whereas for a teacher each September seems to come more quickly than the last, for a fourth grader in May, the previous September is truly a long time ago. For a ten-year-old, far away can mean the other side of the world, but it can also mean a strange neighborhood a few blocks away.

In each chapter Monica describes how she developed and taught a single unit, analyzes sample student work, and reflects on what she and her students learned. Also within each chapter Stephanie contributes three sections: Zooming In, an informational essay on the subject of the unit; Booktalk, reviews of books we felt were especially worthwhile for each unit; and Tools of the Trade, specific tips to help extend the ideas in the chapter. Annotated bibliographies for each unit are provided at the back of the book.

We intend this book to be useful to teachers in different ways. First of all, we hope that the ideas presented will strike a chord in some of you: that the pedagogy, methodology, and reflections will be similar to your own, yet offer something new as well. Additionally, we hope that the projects described will excite you into trying something similar. By no means do we expect you to replicate them exactly as described; however, we do hope that you will be inspired to try variations of them in your own classrooms. The classroom vignettes, the children's work, and Monica's reflections on her own successes and failures may give some of you new insights into the way teachers teach and children learn. Finally, the resources and suggestions provided we hope will make it easier for you to bring more history into your own classroom.

History, the sum of the world's stories, is a massive discipline. So many voices are heard today, and so much clamor as to whose stories should be heard, whose are right, whose are true. Helping children to acquire and use the tools needed to make sense of the cacophony is what our work is all about.

Acknowledgments

My thinking about history, teaching, learning, and children has been immeasurably helped by many people. In particular, I wish to thank past and present colleagues, administrators, and staff at the Dalton School. Peter Sommer encouraged me to go into uncharted territories and Kam Allen supported me once I was in them. Karen Balliett, Tom Doran, Mark Milstein, Pamela Ness, and Steve Tower gave me their ears and ideas as we considered how best to teach social studies to fourth graders. Havelock Hewes and Sarah Gribetz picked up my ideas with enthusiasm and made them into their own; I learned a great deal from them. Librarians Audrey Zucker, Donna Goldberg, and Eileen Sorota delighted in finding the perfect books and multimedia resources for each unit.

Julia Stokien and Virginia Ford were supportive in ways too numerous to mention. Parent and photographer Barbara Julius shot many roles of film to supplement the photographs Stephanie and I had taken.

Thanks to my many students. I learn more from them every year. I am particularly grateful to the members of my 1995–96 and 1996–97 classes who are featured in the following chapters. Some opted for pen names, while others preferred to appear in these pages under their real names.

Thanks to my family: my parents, who provided me with an intellectual environment where thinking about history was built into our lives; my sister, Susan; and her wonderful children, Anna and Benjamin.

Thanks finally to the people of Stenhouse: Philippa Stratton, our exemplary editor, who is an amazing listener; Tom Seavey; and Martha Drury.

Monica Edinger

The path toward this book has been a somewhat unconventional one, and there are many people who provided support along the way. I would like to thank Paula Rubel, Abraham Rosman, and the late Robert F. Murphy for their inspiration both as teachers and writers. Karen Kane, Ann Prewitt, and Heather Nielsen, my colleagues at the American Museum of Natural History, contributed to my thinking about object-based learning and anthropology, and have made work a pleasure. Kay Grennan, an extraordinary volunteer, always took up the challenges I threw at her, most recently proofreading all the bibliographies for this book. Thanks also to Frank Moretti, formerly the Associate Headmaster of the Dalton School, who created the collaboration between the Museum and Dalton and hired me to design the program. I also want to thank Neil Goldberg, a colleague at Dalton and a friend since our days at Columbia; and Claire Curtin, whose passion for writing is always inspirational and whose daily kindnesses mean so much. Thanks also to Joyce Cherubin for all her hard work.

Thanks also to my parents, David and Hilda Fins, and my sister, Deborah, who have always been there to help when needed. My father's lifelong interest in history and my mother's efforts as the maintainer of family traditions have shaped my thinking about the past.

My greatest debt of gratitude goes to my husband, Roy Markowitz, whose passion for his own work in music has been a daily reminder of the importance of the pleasure of work. His support and encouragement enabled me to spend long hours away from him and our son without too much guilt. Finally, I wish to thank my son, David, for his patience and understanding of my absence during the height of baseball season.

Stephanie Fins

CHAPTER ONE

Teaching About the Past

"What is history?" I ask.

"Things that somebody has done to change," ventures Aly.

It is the first day of school, and my students and I are getting to know each other. I know a few by sight: Charles because his sister was in my class several years ago, Spencer because his class visited mine last year. But I don't know Freddie at all; he tells me he is a historian already, an expert on warfare, especially anything "after the Revolution." There is Elana, anxious to make herself known to me, who tells me that history is "things that happened in the past," and David, who defines history as "occurrences of the past." But most of the twenty students sit quietly, not at all sure what to expect from me, from their new classmates, from their new year in school.

Room 909 seems barren this early September morning. Certainly, there are books invitingly displayed, a tidy classroom library with pillows artfully arranged nearby, photos, books, and mementos on or around my desk in the corner. But the walls and bulletin boards are bare, the cubbies empty, the work surfaces blank. There is no sense yet of the young scholars who will be inhabiting this room for the next ten months. To alleviate the unrelenting whiteness of the empty bulletin boards, I have put up fresh red paper—but it will be up to the new occupants of Room 909 to fill the boards with evidence of their learning. And so my twenty new students sit nervously in their new school clothes with one question on their mind. "Will you give us homework today?" they ask again and again.

It will take some time for us to get to know each other, but we will. They will learn that I am a book lover, that I think reading is the most important homework of all. I will learn that Courtney considers herself quiet in school yet talkative at home, that Michael is a fanatic collector of basketball cards, that Jesse leaves early on Thursdays for tennis. They will learn that I am a writer who wants them all to see themselves as writers too. I will learn that Sam can tell me everything about the Yankees, that Spencer is an expert on the Victorian era, that Ali plays the violin, and that Emma loves cats. And they will learn of my passionate interest in history, what it is and how one uses it.

As the year goes on, I'll delight in watching this class come together as a community, observe them develop as independent learners, as peer reviewers, as members of groups. The bulletin boards will fill up, as will the walls, the windows, even the window shades as the documents of our learning multiply. By the end of the year our small ninth floor room will be filled with the artifacts of our learning and thinking: posters of our immigrant *oral histories, file cabinets bulging with student portfolios, and charts everywhere, historical records of our conversations.*

I've been a classroom teacher for over twenty years, a fourth-grade teacher at the Dalton School for the last decade. Dalton is a K–12 private school in New York City, begun over seventy years ago by Helen Parkhurst, a leader in the progressive education movement. Today, the school has a reputation for innovation, and the faculty is fortunate in having a myriad of resources to draw upon when planning instruction. Consultants, specialists, interested colleagues, supportive administrators and parents, a large library, an evolving technology program, museums, and the city itself make curriculum development and teaching a pleasure. The student body is largely upper-middle-class and white, but over 30 percent are on scholarship and there is a commitment at every level of the school to diversify.

When I began teaching fourth grade at Dalton the social studies curriculum was quite traditional. I was given a U.S. history textbook and a map skills workbook that I could use any way I wished. My class completed the map skills workbook quickly, and I focused on the U.S. history text. At that time I was certain that my students needed to learn the facts first, then synthesize them in some sort of creative way. I never questioned the chronological approach to history provided by the textbook, and the actual topics and specific facts presented in the text mattered little to me. It would never have occurred to me to consider abandoning the textbook; it seemed as good a vehicle as any for getting those facts into my students. I focused meticulously on the sequence of each unit in the text, beginning with our study of carefully selected vocabulary words and moving on to oral readings of the textbook, then written answers (complete sentences, please!) to comprehension questions about the text and, finally, projects. I was certain that I excelled at designing and overseeing creative projects. My students dressed up and gave speeches as explorers, wrote poignant letters to England as children during the colonial period, created wonderful quilts of the Revolution, books on western settlement, dioramas of inventions. The projects were fun, and the children left my class extremely proud of themselves. I was also quite pleased with myself. My students appeared to be getting lots of history in a rigorous yet enjoyable and creative way.

After a few years of this, my complacency was shaken by an administrator to whom I'd proudly given a unit on western movement developed by myself and a fellow fourth-grade teacher. As usual, the unit consisted of controlled vocabulary, readings from the text, comprehension questions, and projects at the end. However, I didn't get the response I expected. Rather than complimenting me on my creative curriculum development, the administrator asked why American Indians were so poorly represented in the unit. "What about Manifest Destiny?" he queried. I was taken aback. I took a closer look at the textbook and, indeed, American Indians were superficially treated.

"But—but—" I protested, "I just followed the textbook. What else did you expect?" What he expected, it seemed, was for me to look beyond the textbook in my teaching of U.S. history.

This incident shook me up. I thought I was a very good teacher. My projects were so wonderful, I thought smugly. Everyone liked them. No teacher I knew gave a thought to the information that was or was not in the textbook; we all took the accuracy of the information for granted. And certainly I had not given any thought to a non-textbook approach to American Indians in U.S. history. Frankly, I'd never had any interest in American Indians. And I hadn't thought about where the factual information we used came from, just as long as there was enough of it for us to use in our projects. Textbook or trade book, it made no difference to me.

That summer I went to Taos, New Mexico, to begin to learn something about American Indians firsthand. Once I'd gotten beyond my defensive posturing I recognized that my critic was quite right; the textbook indeed gave a very limited view of American Indians in U.S. history. Suddenly I realized that facts did matter and that I had to do something about expanding the resources I was providing my students. Over the next few years, as I learned more about Native Americans and brought them to the center of my social studies program, I moved away from the textbook. Eventually I dropped it altogether.

During this period I came to know Stephanie, a lecturer and anthropologist at the American Museum of Natural History. Her position at the museum was funded by Dalton; she worked closely with the school's teachers, mostly to customize museum trips. Stephanie was an enthusiastic learner. She became an extraordinary resource for me, seeking out new materials, doing special lessons in my classroom with artifacts and slides from the museum and her own personal collection, and designing our field trips to the museum to fit closely with our classroom work.

The year after my visit to Taos, I stuck with the traditional U.S. history curriculum, simply tacking on a new unit in September, "The First People in the Americas." Before long I revamped the curriculum to focus primarily on Native Americans. I moved far beyond the textbook, using a huge range of resources from trade books to magazines to videos to artifacts to museum collections. The units became far more open-ended. I dispensed with the controlled vocabulary and oral readings and jumped right to the projects. Now my students were creating posters of Anasazi cliff dwellings, books on the Pueblo, and models of ancient Maya cities. My curriculum had moved from a textbook-based program that emphasized "objective" historical facts to one that was trade-book-based and emphasized a deeper understanding of the people under study. My hope was that the facts that my students were learning were more accurate than those in the textbook and would provide them with a basis for a more well-rounded view of Native Americans in U.S. history.

It took a special exhibit at the museum to change my thinking once again. In the fall of 1992, Stephanie urged me to consider a unit on the Northwest Coast that would tie in with the museum's special exhibit, "Chiefly Feasts: The Enduring Kwakiutl Potlatch." I was reluctant at first. It seemed to me that we were doing enough with Indians. My units on the Southwest, Plains, and Maya were going well; why include another group? Stephanie kept pressing me, and I finally succumbed to her enthusiasm. In November I attended a workshop at the museum on the Kwakiutl and began reading all I could on the native people of the Northwest Coast. As I did so I became intrigued by the way their history is known. On the one hand there are the written records and photographs of outsiders; on the other there are the stories and art of the tribes themselves. With that revelation I developed a unit for my students: "The Northwest Coast Indians: Creating History and Myth." No doubt I should have recognized the complexities of history as maintained in different cultures as we had learned about the Anasazi and the Maya, but I hadn't. It was only while learning about the Northwest Coast people that the issue of who tells history and how it is told became significant to me. As we worked through the unit I began to observe my own fourth graders grappling with the idea of history. What did they think history was? Were they able to recognize the subjective nature of historical texts? What did they make of cultures that had no written histories? Could they acknowledge themselves as respectful outsiders when studying the history of a distant culture?

My interest led me to invite my students to become historians working as scholars: doing oral histories, writing firsthand accounts of potentially significant historical events, puzzling over documents and artifacts, researching secondary sources, considering the subjective nature of the information they had uncovered and how to interpret it. Our subjects have ranged from ourselves to living immigrants to distant cultures to people of other eras.

What Is History?

My September fourth graders offer a reasonable definition of history; to them it is clearly the past. This is a safe definition to offer their new teacher, one that they have determined based on the way the word has been used around them: by parents, friends, relatives, teachers, in books, in the media. After all, my own dictionary defines history as "the branch of knowledge dealing with past events." Yet I expect that as my students receive new information on history this year, as they discuss ideas about history with each other and with me, and as they reflect on the idea of history, their definition will alter and shift, becoming deeper and more complex as they learn more. And I will be doing the same thing. I continually seek out definitions of history; I consider the word's use in new books on the subject, in the media, by my students, by colleagues, friends, and relatives. As I take in new information, talk about it, and reflect on it, my definition shifts too. No longer do I consider history to be important political events of the past determined by experts far removed from me. I've broadened my personal definition to include my own past, the acts of ordinary people of the past, elements of myth, conflicting stories, and interpretation.

Most recently, I've become intrigued about the way the term is used in the media, especially in sports reportage. At every opportunity, the 1996 Olympic commentators referred to events as historic. So too was the Yankees' triumph in the 1996 World Series. How do I use this view of history? These events are now in the past, but are they significant? To athletes, no doubt they are. But what about the rest of us? What does that kind of history have to do with the kind of history we consider in school? I'm not quite sure, but I'm paying close attention and using this new information to rework my personal definition of history.

For me, history is not a set idea, but an evolving one, something that we all are continually determining for ourselves. Tom Holt, in *Thinking Historically* (1990), defines history as "past human experience recollected. Thus our own everyday experience is the substance of history: our individual life cycles, our family's or community's stories, the succession of generations. To construct coherent stories about this collective experience—something we all do—is to create histories" (p. 9).

My Goals

Like all teachers, like all adults involved with children, I have hopes for my students—ideas, thoughts, and knowledge that I hope they will leave with at the end of their fourth-grade year with me. My goals are optimistic. They aren't simple or easy to assess. I don't think I can ever know for sure if all my students have or have not met these goals. Certainly, I can and do set up tasks, questions, and ways to assess my students' development toward achieving these goals. However, I may have students who are beginning to achieve a goal, but who cannot yet articulate or demonstrate this. My goals are continuous; all I can do is watch my students, see if some of them are meeting the goals, and consider what to do to continually help them all.

The following are my goals for my students:

- I want my students to construct evolving personal definitions of history.
- I want my students to see themselves as historians, to know that they can create stories of the past just as the experts do.
- I want my students to be skeptical about facts of the past, to recognize that this information has been collected, interpreted, and presented by real people who have varying points of view.
- I want my students to be able to generalize about similar aspects of the past while still recognizing the uniqueness of each event.
- I want my students to see history as real.
- I want my students to use historical stories to help themselves develop as empathetic, ethical, and moral beings.
- I want my students to see purpose in studying history, to see how knowing the past affects their present and future.
- I want my students to be inspired, delighted, and intrigued by the past.
- I want my students to discover new things about the past, new ways of thinking, new ideas, and new interpretations that amaze us all.
- I want my students to take pleasure in their study of history.

Content Quandaries

Curriculum content is an ongoing issue for us teachers, a quagmire of endless dilemmas. How I wish that it could all be settled, that someone would give me the magic solution to all this contention and controversy! The arguments have been going on forever. From Plato to Rousseau, from Hirsch to my hairdresser—everyone seems to have an opinion as to what I should teach. I read professional journals, newspapers, and books. I listen to, argue, and talk with colleagues. I watch and listen to children. Through all that, I have three concerns when considering what content to teach: outside demands, children's interests, and my own passions.

Outside Demands

A friend recently complained to me that her daughter, a third grader at another progressive school in the city, knew nothing about American history. I responded, "Why should she? It hasn't been in her school experience. And does it matter? She'll learn about it soon enough." My friend wasn't appeased, and I knew why. I too have been surprised at gaps in my students' general knowledge. It comes up unexpectedly. Beginning a study of early Native Americans I give my students an outline map of North America and ask them to mark where New York City is. My intention is to have them see how far they live from the lands of the Kwakiutl, the Pueblo, and the Maya, people we will be studying this year. However, I have to stop as children place New York City in Newfoundland, in Rhode Island, even in Florida. I don't blame them or their previous teachers. It just hasn't come up till now. Why should they know? And it only takes a moment for me to set them straight. At another time (during the 1996 governmental shutdown) our morning meeting runs over as I try, in response to a child's question, to explain the complex relationship between the President and Congress. The students are hungry for specifics, trying to make sense of what they see on television and hear from the adults around them. Yet while some want to know more, others look bored, ready to get to their own work of the day, work that has nothing to do with the government. However I handle such a situation, I always end up feeling uncertain and unsatisfied.

E. D. Hirsch would argue that the solution is a curriculum consisting of established factual knowledge. In his 1996 book *The Schools We Need and Why We Don't Have Them*, he argues for a carefully constructed national curriculum full of factual information upon which children can build year after year. He points out that all children need to be in school with the same "intellectual capital" and that those not from upper-middle-class backgrounds often lack elements of this intellectual capital. Thus, one child may know who Cinderella is because the story was read at home, while another might not because no bedtime story was provided in her environment. Hirsch's argument makes sense, but how can he be sure what information is most important to know and how to present it? His "core knowledge" children's books consist of excerpts, abridgments, and adaptations—none of which encourages in-depth study.

Others tell me not to worry. What is important, they say, is knowing how to find the information and interpret it, not the information itself. There is a massive amount to know out there. Multiculturalists and traditionalists go head to head as to what information should be in a United States history course. Those of us doing the actual teaching are caught in the middle. I feel that way all the time. How can I provide my students with the information they need, and what is that information?

My solution has been less than satisfactory. I look at what is generally taught to fourth graders, see what the other teachers in my school are teaching, listen to parents, listen to children. From that I make decisions as to what the content will be. And I try to stay flexible and alert to unanticipated situations, gaps, and questions, making snap decisions as to how much to veer from the plan of the day, whether it matters for my students to know what I realize they don't know, skipping over, moving on.

Children's Interests

Freddie is a budding paleontologist and is also fascinated by martial history. Elana is absorbed by the Holocaust, reading book after book about it. All my students are full of individual interests, and their lives are so busy that I frequently worry that they don't have enough time to explore their passions. I provide them with a thematic curriculum, one that offers a lot of choices, but with a content mandated by me. And it so happens that wars, dinosaurs, and the Holocaust aren't central to my curriculum.

I am never totally sure what is meant by the term "child-centered." Aren't all teachers and schools child-centered? After all, we teachers, whatever our style, are forced to focus on children all day. Schools are full of children—how can a school be anything but child-centered? I'd like to think of my teaching as child-centered—my students fill the room with their activity and noise, and they are certainly the center of my life in the classroom. It seems to me that the opposite of child-centered would be teacher-centered, a classroom where the children are always focused on the teacher. But while I don't stand before my students lecturing them, I do make the major decisions regarding curriculum. I decide on themes, materials, and projects. I feel comfortable doing so, because I am the experienced person.

I struggle to balance the children's interests with mine and the school's. If I think there is particular content my students should indeed know, how do I balance that belief with my desire to help students study what personally interests them? At my school, students are busy all day. The children go off after school to religious school, music lessons, and sports. They don't have a lot of time to investigate their passions, either in school or out. One attempt I have made to encourage individual interests is to create a program called Explorations. Children can decide to do an Exploration outside of school at any time, or in school when they have finished assigned work. I have had children investigate a British monarch, stadia, and the basis of the English language. For those less motivated, the best I can do is to show my personal interest in each of them and lead them to books and materials about their personal passions while at the same time encouraging them in their work with the class.

Teacher Passions

I spent two years as a Peace Corps Volunteer in Sierra Leone, West Africa. Subsequently I took a master's degree in international education. I have photos, slides, books, and artifacts, not to mention memories of stories about my time in Africa. Unfortunately, only once in my many years of teaching was I able to teach a unit on Sierra Leone. Somehow Africa never fit into the curriculum.

I've learned that most of what I am required to teach can be interesting. I began learning about Native Americans under administrative pressure; today I'm perceived at my school as an expert, even an activist, about them. But how does a teacher's particular passion and special knowledge come into his or her teaching? What happens, for example, when my friend is passionate about the Middle Ages, but he teaches eighth grade and the Middle Ages is officially part of our sixth-grade curriculum? My solution has been to give the official curriculum priority and try to make it my passion. However, I think this is a weak solution, one that often means that students lose out.

My Practice: Ideas and Theories

All my lofty teaching goals and my struggles with curricular content would be meaningless without determining how they actually play out in the classroom. My colleagues may see me as a thinker and an intellectual, but most of all I enjoy being with children. Over the years I've had opportunities to leave classroom teaching. I began as an art teacher and immediately decided that I hated teaching many classes of different children, that what I wanted to do was work intensively with one group of children for an extended period of time. I made that decision over twenty years ago and have been a classroom teacher ever since. Over those twenty years I have evolved in my teaching as I've watched children and other experienced teachers, as I've read and studied at institutes of higher learning, as I've tried out new theories and ideas in my classroom. My practice is continually evolving, just as my definition of history. The more I learn, the more my teaching changes. The following theories and ideas currently underpin much of what goes on in my classroom.

The Writing Process

I first became familiar with the writing process in 1984 when I attended Lucy Calkins' Summer Writing Institute at Teachers College, Columbia University. It was a revelation for me because I had an obsession with helping children to write well. Throughout my childhood I had been very proud of my writing. I was a miserable speller, but my teachers never allowed me to feel that that was all there was to writing. I was also a voracious reader and in high school was placed in history and English Advanced Placement courses. The fall of my senior year my English teacher told my parents that he felt I should not be involved in any extracurricular activities because I needed to improve my writing. I was devastated. I had no idea what he thought was wrong with my writing, and I have no memory of him showing me. I only remember staying up into the early morning hours trying desperately to revise my work and only making it worse. In college I was sent to a remedial writing tutor who told me my problem was all emotional. That may well have been the case; nonetheless, I stayed away from English courses throughout my undergraduate and graduate education, preferring to gain my knowledge of English literature on my own. When I began teaching I was intent on keeping my students from having an experience like mine. However, I was always unsatisfied with how I was teaching writing until I attended the Institute.

At the time, I was teaching sixth-grade social studies, and as a result of my exposure to the idea of the writing process I immediately turned my teaching of research report writing upside down. It was easy to do. I dropped the formal plan I had previously followed that required students to follow a lock-step procedure: take notes, write an outline, write a draft, revise it, write a final draft. Instead I encouraged them to research, write, and rewrite in their own way until their research pieces were all they wanted them to be. When I moved to fourth grade I continued to use a writing process approach. I have refined my methods over the years as I've watched my students, read more, attended conferences, talked to others, and started to write myself. All the projects described in this book have a writing component, and all were done using a writing process approach to teaching and learning.

Political Teaching

On the day of the O. J. Simpson verdict, my students came dashing into the classroom, bursting to talk about it, aborting my plan to continue our work on the Northwest Coast Native Americans. Of course we talked about the verdict—that day. But by the end of the week we were back to our focus on Kwakiutl life. A lost opportunity? I wonder. Perhaps I should have ditched the unit and used the moment to focus on the issue at hand: race in America.

For many years now I've subscribed to a remarkable publication out of Milwaukee, Wisconsin, called *Rethinking Schools.* The articles are often angry and strong—rebuffing a school voucher attempt, strongly resisting efforts to maintain tracking, arguing always for the awareness of politics in education. In a 1994 special publication, *Rethinking Our Classrooms: Teaching for Equity and Justice,* the editors, Bill Bigelow, Linda Christensen, Stan Karp, Barbara Miner, and Bob Peterson, write, "*Rethinking Our Classrooms* begins from the premise that schools and classrooms should be laboratories for a more just society than the one we now live in" (p. 4). These activists argue for curriculum content to come from the children and from political issues. I am certain that they would see no conflict for me regarding the O. J. Simpson verdict. They would expect me to drop my curriculum and take the issue of race as far as it needed to go; the Native Americans could wait. But I'm not so sure. Maybe they could wait, or maybe they would drop out of sight. What if we switch to race in America and my students never do an in-depth study of a Native American culture? I worry that they will miss out on something, that one political teaching decision will be at the expense of another. The best I can hope for is that I model passionate activism for my students; through my being political my classroom is political as well.

Project-Based Learning

I love projects—always have, always will. When I was a child I loved projects: constructing a tiny house in the woods for fairies, crocheting a pot holder, producing a play in the basement with my friends. Sometimes my projects were for school: a sugar cube model of an ancient Egyptian farm, a poster for English class. There was always something very special for me about working hard on something and eventually seeing it as a final product. As an undergraduate I majored in art and veered between two interests: printmaking and children's book illustration. After graduation I decided to teach, pursuing a career in illustration on the side. Whatever I did as an artist had a project component. I did series of etchings and engravings based on themes. I illustrated Kipling's "The Elephant's Child," several classic fairy tales, and a few original stories of my own. I enjoyed the idea of a larger construct within which to do my work.

I've always done my best learning with projects, so it seemed only right that it would be the way I would teach. No matter where I have taught, I have always found a way to build my teaching around projects.

One of the reasons I came to Dalton was that project-based learning was an integral part of the school's philosophy. The Dalton Plan was developed by the school's founder, Helen Parkhurst, and contains an element called the Assignment. The Assignment is meant to be a course of study that children can follow with great independence. It is to be structured in a way that allows children to move deeper into the subject, if that is their desire. At Dalton today we argue constantly about the nature of the Assignment. Some teachers believe the subject should be child-selected; others believe that it needs to be teacher-driven. What I like best about the concept is that it encourages project-based learning. Parkhurst's own book, *Education on the Dalton Plan* (1922), includes several Assignments that include extremely creative projects.

Imaginative Learning

"Imagination is more important than knowledge," stated Albert Einstein, one of the world's most creative thinkers. He said this as a rebuke to his own nineteenth-century teachers, who most likely would have argued just the opposite: that knowledge is far more important than imagination. Kieran Egan, in his book *Imagination in Teaching and Learning* (1992), defines imagination as "the capacity to think of things as possibly being so; it is an intentional act of mind; it is the source of invention, novelty, and generativity; it is not implicated in all perception and in the construction of all meaning; it is not distinct from rationality but is rather a capacity that greatly enriches rational thinking" (p. 43).

To me, imagination is a wonderful thing. As a child, I lived a vivid fantasy life. My sister and I could play for hours in the backyard pretending we were squirrels in our nests of pine needles or in Oz searching for the Wicked Witch of the West. I recall reading history books and fantasizing what it might be like living in ancient Rome or Greece. To know history in any substantive way, it seems to me, is to utilize the imagination. How can we make sense of the past if we cannot imagine it as real? I attempt in my teaching to create learning situations that encourage the activation of imaginative thinking. Often such thinking results in creative, unexpected, and novel ideas.

Nowadays, with the sudden burst of information available to us via new technologies, it is important to remember that information still needs to be worked with, considered imaginatively to be made new and different. I attempt to provide an environment where students' imaginations are encouraged to flourish.

■ ■ ■

"And if history is the past, what do you think the past is?" I ask my new students.

"Yesterday or a long time ago," states Nathaniel.

"Anytime before the present" is Chris's idea.

"Something that happened and can't again" is Amanda's final word on the subject.

"So at this point in the year, we all can at least agree that history is the past, which is something that happened sometime before today and can't happen again," I note as I finish writing all the ideas on a large sheet of chart paper. Carefully, I note the date at the top: September 6, 1996. "This is our class's very first historical document, a record of our first conversation about history. Not only is it about history, but it *is* history—our history as learners this year." I jot down the last words at the bottom of the chart and stick it up on the wall. Already the room looks less bare.

 # Zooming In

What Is Historiography?

Historiography is the study of how history is conceptualized and taught, including the study of historical methods and approaches to interpretation. When thinking about teaching history, it is important to remember that historians disagree about why events happened and how they should be analyzed. There has been considerable debate about what historical analysis should include, about the primacy of one kind of history over another, and about how to establish priorities. Over time there has been a shift away from a chronological approach to teaching history that stressed memorization in favor of analysis of historical periods.

Certain approaches to teaching history that have been developed in reaction to traditional approaches are often referred to as "new history." While traditional history focused primarily on politics, new history is concerned with a wider range of human activity. New history is also less interested in the activities of "great men" and more interested in the experiences of ordinary people. Other changes include use of a wider variety of evidence, including visual and oral evidence, and a greater concern with consideration of varied and opposing points of view.

While a review of all of the issues of historiography falls beyond the scope of this book, it is important to be aware of the discussions taking place within the academic discipline of history that will ultimately influence the way teachers are taught and the way history is taught in schools.

Booktalk

What Is History Teaching?
by Chris Husbands

Looking for a reference that bridges the gap between academic history and classroom practice? *What Is History Teaching?* by Chris Husbands, a British historian and an experienced classroom teacher, raises many critical issues regarding the teaching of history and provides many thought-provoking suggestions. In clear and concise chapters, Husbands examines developments within academic history, explores the ways in which language conveys ideas about history, and discusses both the role of story in history and the importance of imagination in the development of historical understanding. The second half of the book focuses on teaching practice, on the ways in which classroom work can be designed to encourage historical understanding. The book's central focus is the issue of how students learn history and how teachers can enhance the development of historical thinking. Husbands advocates using a variety of strategies and discusses the importance of allowing students time to investigate a subject. He suggests ways teachers can encourage students to talk extensively about a historical topic and ways they can engage them in writing and role playing, all of which provide students with a range of opportunities to develop and share their ideas while mastering necessary skills. Husbands also devotes a chapter to assessment, in which he stresses the importance of creating opportunities for self-assessment that are meaningful, but not overly burdensome to students or teachers. Always interesting, this book challenges the reader to think deeply about the way we teach and learn about the past.

National Standards for History
published by the National Center for the Study of History in Schools, UCLA

As you think about teaching history and what students learn, it might be of interest to look at *National Standards for History* (Nash and Crabtree 1996), a volume that encompasses the teaching of history from kindergarten through high school. An outgrowth of the movement to set national standards for subject content, these history standards, developed by a panel of historians under the auspices of the University of California at Los Angeles, outline specific goals for teaching both world history and American history. The intent was to have teachers, schools, and states use national standards in developing curriculum and state curriculum frameworks.

The publication of the original standards in 1994 released a storm of controversy about what should be taught as history. While there was general agreement that Americans were poorly educated on the subject of history, the suggested solutions to correct the problem were contested. While both sets of standards were controversial, the U.S. history standards evoked the strongest criticism. Particularly controversial was the idea that attention paid to western history be reduced in order to expand the time spent on Asian, African, and pre-Columbian history. The teaching examples provided in both volumes were heavily criticized as being biased and excessively concerned with multiculturalism.

Leaders on both sides of the political spectrum took up the debate, citing examples from the lengthy document to make their points about what should be taught in our schools. The Senate joined in, censuring the standards despite the defense of many prominent historians. As a result of the controversy and to address the criticisms, two panels were convened, which revised the standards. The revised edition contains many changes, but retained the original mission of broadening the content of history teaching and helping teachers develop a framework that would enhance students' critical thinking skills. All of the examples were removed, as was much of the language that was criticized as too judgmental. While many of the conservative critics were satisfied with the revisions, some of the original authors continued to defend the original standards.

Excerpts from the standards, as well as discussions of the controversy surrounding them, can be found on-line, by doing a Web search with the words "national history standards." Articles from several major newspapers and magazines, postings by historians on listservs, and references to publications not available on-line can all be accessed.

Tools of the Trade

Collaborating with a Museum

Educational outreach programs, with teacher workshops and programs for school groups, have long been a part of most museums' offerings. For many years the relationship between teachers and museum educators tended to be somewhat informal, with individual teachers and museum educators coming together to create programs that varied from year to year. Within the last decade, however, there has been a major shift, as schools and museums work together to create new partnerships and long-term relationships.

As you think about integrating museums or historical societies into your classroom curriculum, you might want to consider exploring the possibility of a long-term partnership with a cultural institution in your area. Although the development of such partnerships takes time and requires administrative support, sometimes ideas for collaboration come directly out of the needs of individual classroom teachers. As you investigate the external resources available to you, it may be worthwhile to inquire about the possibilities of such collaborations. Many collaborations develop out of a particular teacher's need to find resources to support a new curriculum initiative.

Finding an institutional partner may not be as difficult as you think. As cultural institutions look for more ways to expand their audience, as museum educators explore the range of educational resources they can offer to schools and work to develop programs that are more than add-ons to existing school curricula, there may be opportunities for new partnerships. Look also for existing activities that you can join, such as teachers' focus groups, summer workshops held at cultural institutions, and extended field trips for teachers sponsored by cultural institutions and universities.

It may also be worth exploring the activities being developed at some of the museum magnet schools around the country, such as the Museum Magnet School in St. Paul, Minnesota, and the New York City Museum School in New York. Descriptions of some of these schools may be found through the Internet.

As interactive communication networks continue to develop, look for new opportunities for distance learning available through satellite television transmission and through resources being developed for the World Wide Web. Most cultural institutions have Web sites mounted, and some are beginning to include activities that link to various topics related to their collections.

Learning to Look

Just as students need to learn how to read verbal information, they also need to learn how to interpret visual information. There are many approaches you can take to helping children improve their visual literacy. If you plan on using visual material as a form of historical evidence, practice with simple objects can strengthen the skills students will use when interpreting objects.

Begin by analyzing a single object. Select either a familiar object or an object that is unknown to the students; it need not be exotic. You can develop your own strategies for approaching working with objects, or draw on published descriptions of activities designed to practice object-based learning. An activity developed around a paper clip, described in a wonderful resource for museum field trips, *Teach the Mind, Touch the Spirit: A Guide to Focused Field Trips* (Voris, Sedzielarz, Blackmon 1986), provides an example of how to generate discussion and engage learners with an everyday object. An activity designed around a McDonald's box, described in an article entitled "Teaching Yourself to Teach with Objects" (Shuh 1982) and widely circulated among museum educators, is also useful. While these two exercises begin with different objects, there are many similarities in the approaches taken. More than forty questions are suggested for each activity, each focusing on different aspects of inquiry. Viewers are asked to describe the characteristics of the object that would help someone who has never seen one to understand it and how it is used. They are told to smell it; to feel it; to draw it; to think about what they know about the history of the object, its availability, and its cost; to speculate as to how the object is made; to write creatively about the journey of the object through its lifetime. These are just a few of the ways that are suggested as ways of coming to know and analyze an object. The point of both of these exercises is to help teachers feel comfortable providing their students with opportunities to learn from objects, something teachers may have little training or experience with themselves.

It is important that you try out an observational activity such as those just suggested so that you become comfortable working with objects on your own before you try it with a class. While it may be useful for teachers to begin with a few questions that they have generated, each class will come up with their own questions about objects that they may want to explore. Have students begin by making careful observations, describing attributes, drawing the object, and writing about it. Are the children most interested in the use of the object, discussing how it was developed and made, or in creating stories or imaginary histories for the object?

A follow-up activity involves working with a group of objects that are almost identical, but with some minor differences. For example, select thirty bananas. The bananas are placed together and each student selects one. The students examine their bananas closely, from every angle. Depending on their age and abilities, you may ask them to make notes or drawings of their bananas. After they have spent about ten to twenty minutes examining their bananas, the bananas are then regrouped. The students are then asked to find their own banana in the group. Did the notes or drawings they made help them? Ask the students to review their experiences with this exercise. As a class, discuss what made the exercise easy or difficult. Almost any kind of everyday object could be chosen—well-used pencils or keys are other possibilities.

For the next lesson, select items that are less familiar. Collect an assortment of objects, such as kitchen utensils, craft tools, or hardware, that are likely to be unfamiliar to the majority of the students. Each student then selects one item to study. Have students closely examine the objects, noting attributes, materials, and design elements. Have them hypothesize as to the objects' function. Each student presents his or her findings to the class, and any students who have additional ideas should be invited to present their views.

The point of these activities is to have students develop their visual acuity, to develop their language skills and thought processes while working with objects, and to encourage creativity. Classroom experience with objects will be particularly useful if you will be working with objects from museums or other institutions.

Analysis of visual evidence can be a way of getting students to think about the kinds of questions historians ask of objects. It can lead them to think about the kinds of inferences that can be made from a single object as opposed to a group of objects and help develop their ability to generate and test hypotheses based on visual data.

Researching On-Line

For each chapter of the book, we present relevant on-line resources that can be used in historical research. Through on-line resources, you and your students can connect to libraries and facilities far from the classroom. Lesson plans can be shared, research can be conducted, and images can be downloaded. You can make virtual tours of historic places.

While there are many sources that can be recommended, the sites we present were selected with an eye to what would be available for a reasonable period of time. The focus is primarily on sites that are maintained by large cultural institutions, such as universities, museums, and government organizations. Many Web sites mounted by individuals appear for a short period of time, but are removed when the authors decide to create a CD-ROM or no longer maintain the site. As you review these sources, check for links to other sites. Also, keep in mind that the sites may have moved or disappeared the next time you go to them.

An excellent Web site with a broad range of historical material is the Library of Congress National Digital Library, American Memory Collection. This site seeks to make the library's collection of documents, films, manuscripts, photographs, and recordings available to a wide audience. Historical collections on the site include an interesting assortment of multimedia collections, with African American pamphlets; photographs from the Civil War; documents relating to the Harlem Renaissance; materials from the Farm Security Administration and the Office of War Information from 1938 to 1944; photographs of transportation around the world taken from 1894 to 1896; and life history manuscripts from the WPA Federal Writers' Project on folklore. Many other collections are in progress and will be available in the near future; these include first-person narratives from California, Michigan, Minnesota, and Wisconsin; Presidential papers; and surveys of architecture and engineering. The site also contains lesson plans for educators to help them use the various collections.

Another site that has led to many interesting links is entitled "History and Social Studies Web Sites for K–12 Teachers." Written by Dennis Boals, the site is designed to facilitate the use of the Internet by teachers. The page lists sites on a broad range of historical topics. Through this location you can find linkages to sites on American, European, and non-Western history as well as archaeology, oral history, and genealogy. Some sites are designed specifically for students. One of the links made through this page turned up an excellent list of history pages, as well as a sampler of more than twenty definitions of history written by a wide range of people including James Joyce, Karl Marx, and Henry Ford. Almost a random selection, they were selected, according to the page's author Steve Kreis, to stimulate a reader's historical imagination.

For a discussion of the growing importance of on-line resources for teaching history, see Bill Tally's article "History Goes Digital: Teaching When the Web Is in the Classroom," published in several versions and listed as a Web site below.

The following are some useful Web sites for approaching the study of history:

American Memory: http://lcweb2.loc.gov/ammem/
History and Social Studies Web Sites for K-12 Teachers:
   http://www.execpc.com/~dboals
Resources for Historians: http://www.pagesz.net/~stevek/resources.html
What Is History? A Sampler: http://www.pagesz.net/~stevek/history.html
Bill Tally article: http://www.dlib.org/dlib/september96/09tally.html

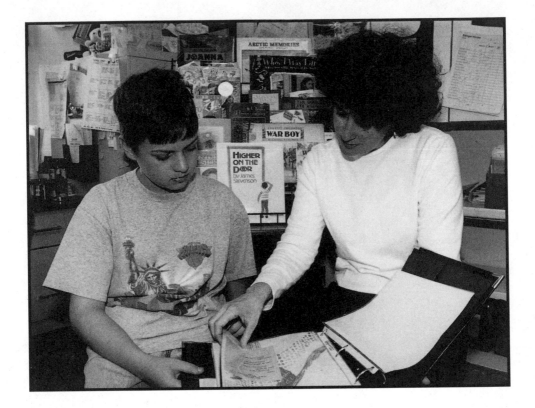

CHAPTER TWO

My Story:
Personal Histories

Richard, a fifth grader, and I are sitting in my classroom after school paging through his portfolio from the previous year, "My Life in Fourth Grade," and reminiscing. "Oh, look at that, Richard! I see that you put in your green card from the first day of school! Oh, and right behind it is your illustration of your journey from the lower school to the middle school. I love the way you made the avenues bodies of water full of boats. Just as if you had really crossed a sea instead of Park Avenue!"

"Well, it was a big journey since Little Dalton is so different from Big Dalton."

I had invited Richard to come back and reflect on his memories of fourth grade because it had been a good year for both of us. Richard had been a very serious student, interested in all that we did. A highly disciplined writer, he felt that he had learned a lot about writing during his year with me.

His portfolio had been created during the final weeks of fourth grade. The children were all asked to look through their collected work of the year. Most of it was in their working portfolios, but additional materials were in notebooks and journals, and on the bulletin boards. I did not tell them what to put in their final fourth-grade portfolios, nor did I suggest what to call them. However, we talked at length about the future value of the portfolios as documents of fourth grade. With this understanding, the children looked at their work with an eye to what was most significant to them— their own histories. Some chose to put in every draft of a piece of writing, and some included only the final, published version. Others photocopied favorite pages from their response journals. Richard had taken on the task with a sense of great responsibility and created a portfolio that was truly a record of what was significant and important to him in fourth grade. Looking at it months later is a trip down a pleasant memory lane.

"There is your author's blurb about Gabe."

"I put it in because Gabe became one of my best friends."

I continue to page through the portfolio.

"Wow, here's all the stuff from your oral history project, from the transcript to your final self-evaluation."

"I learned a lot about my mom and Chile. The only problem was she had a problem putting action in."

"Well, I think you did a wonderful job adding the action yourself through the illustrations. Now here are your notes and drafts for the Northwest Coast research report on canoes. I remember how much everyone

enjoyed that project. Ah, your Cinderella story. I had forgotten that you wrote two completely different versions. I'll always remember your rat hero's crooked tail becoming permanently straightened at the end."

It is wonderful looking through Richard's portfolio almost a year later. It has become what I hoped it would be: a personal, historical record of his fourth-grade year.

No history can be more immediate than our own. If history can be seen as narrative, the stories of our own past are the historical events that are the most emotional, memorable, and significant to us. Throughout my teaching career I have sought out opportunities for children to bring their own histories to school even as they discover and explore the histories of other times and places. Often this would happen informally, such as when a child spoke at the morning meeting about a fire in his building the night before. Sometimes I would structure more formal engagements, such as personal time lines, autobiographical writing, and other such projects. Additionally, I would encourage children to continually consider their own histories as learners. At the beginning of the year I ask each child to create a learner's profile—a document of his or her previous history as a learner. Frequent self-evaluations throughout the year then became additional records of the children's growth as learners—their history in fourth grade. Richard's portfolio was his carefully constructed history of fourth grade.

Over the last few years, as history has become more central to my teaching, I have looked for ways to provide my students with opportunities to construct historical understanding through personal experiences. Doing an oral history interview, rather than relying on secondary sources, made learning about immigration a personal experience. One year during our Northwest Coast study a colleague and I procured a PTA grant that enabled us to bring a Kwakiutl artist to our school all the way from British Columbia. She made the distant culture and history of the Kwakiutl and other Northwest Coast native peoples more real than anything we could do by ourselves in New York City. Telling the children that they were all her grandchildren, Marion Hunt Doig, with her stories, dances, and artifacts, offered the children a personal connection to an otherwise distant and alien culture. Yet most of all it is the children's own experiences, their own stories and memories, that I have found make learning about the past most real and most alive.

It was during the 1995–96 school year that historical thinking became a central theme in my teaching. I built into each social studies unit a major focus on history. Continually I challenged the children to consider and reconsider what their definition of history was and if it had changed, what historical information is, and what the nature of primary and secondary sources is. While personal experiences were at the forefront of our discussions all year, two special occurrences made personal history particularly significant in advancing the children's historical thinking. The first was an unexpected event: the Blizzard of 1996; the other was a rethinking of a unit on memoir that I had taught many times previously.

My Goals

I have several goals in encouraging my students to explore their personal histories:

- Seeing themselves as part of the flow of history by writing about their own experiences will help my students deepen their personal definitions of history.
- They will see themselves as historians in writing their own personal histories, and the history will feel real to them because they experienced the stories personally.
- Through personal explorations of the past I hope that my students will note the difficulties in determining certain facts of the past, and that they will better understand that history is written by individuals with points of views and opinions.
- Most of all, my hope is that their personal explorations of the past will inspire my students to think deeply and creatively.

The Blizzard of '96

"New York Shut by Worst Storm in 48 Years; East is Buried, Virginia to Massachusetts" was the *New York Times* banner headline on Tuesday, January 9, 1996. It was the day after our winter break; we were supposed to return to school that day, but instead we usually jaded New Yorkers were wandering our empty streets in awe, sledding, taking pictures, building snowmen, and generally having a grand time with a most unexpected natural event. I was highly amused by all the fuss, having spent my childhood in Michigan, where such a storm would have raised hardly an eyebrow. But in New York City it was an amazing and wonderful event. Headline after headline referred to the storm as "one for the history books" and of "historic" proportions. The news media were full of how people spent their days shoveling out mountains of snow to find their cars or cross-country skiing down Fifth Avenue. Noticing all the interviews with people who had been in New York for the Blizzard of 1947, I decided to take advantage of the situation when school finally reopened a few days later.

"So, what did you do the last few days?" I asked. "It was amazing, wasn't it? When I looked down Broadway I couldn't see any cars. It looked like a picture of New York City from a hundred years ago. And it was so quiet without the cars. What an amazing experience!"

"We had to walk so much because we couldn't drive!"

"I went sledding and we made a fort the size of a castle."

"We were on a plane coming back from Florida, and I heard the woman behind me say she had never seen snow before. Boy, was she in for a surprise!"

"I saw people carrying groceries out of a store on a sled!"

"Did you see all the news coverage?" I asked. "The *New York Times* had an editorial where they wrote, 'These days are an Event, a Milestone—like the legendary Blizzards of 1888 and 1947—exclamation points in history.' What do you think of that? You're eyewitnesses to a historical exclamation point! You absolutely must write down your memories of this storm. For the future. For your grandchildren. In case the next big storm is in fifty years and they want to hear from people who were there for the Blizzard of '96. We'll start by making a chart listing everything we remember about the storm." And here is what we wrote.

Things We Noticed and Did During the Storm

Watching television

Bread section empty in the market except for bread crumbs

Watching a man leave the supermarket with his groceries on a sled

Standing on a mountain that was a car

Streets with no moving vehicles

Cleaned out video stores

Pizza delivery

Skiing on the street

Quiet

No cars moving

Digging out car jobs

People helping people

Plows making bigger mountains

Car uncovered by play
Slipping on ice
Ice and snow sculptures
Sledding
Snowbound
Igloos
Staying home
No transportation

With tremendous excitement the children went to work crafting their own first-person accounts of the Blizzard of '96. The final pieces were posted on a bulletin board along with our original list and news articles. This unexpected opportunity provided us with material that became part of the history of our class that year as well as part of each child's personal history and the history of New York City.

Richard's blizzard story, like those of many of his classmates, became part of his portfolio:

The Storm of '96

The Big Mountain

On Monday the eighth of January, my little brother and I went out and threw snowballs at each other. Fifteen minutes later I spotted a giant mountain of fresh fallen snow. We ran over and jumped in the mountain. It was up to my waist and I wasn't even close to touching the ground.

Quick Falling Snow

Right after going to the mountain we went to a spot where the snow was thin and I brushed the snow off and in about two minutes it was covered again. That is how quick the snow was falling.

The Pizza Delivery

My brother and I were playing in the snow, throwing balls at each other, making snow angels and sticking our heads totally into the snow. It didn't feel cold because we had hats and neck warmers.

About one hour later we saw a Domino's pizza delivery man walking straight into the blowing snow and wind. I thought the pizza might freeze.

Asked why he wrote the story, Richard replied, "Because when the last blizzard was in New York they had a lot [of] like paragraphs they took from people and put it in the newspaper." It was history for Richard because "there wouldn't be another one for a while. You asked us to write about what we saw or what we did when it happened."

Richard and I were talking about his story a year after the event, yet he spoke about the blizzard as if it had happened yesterday. "I went out for two days. And since there isn't snow [usually] and whenever there is my little brother and I always try to go out and play in it. So we went outside and we started throwing snowballs at each other and then we saw by a wall that there was a big hill and we jumped into it and I was thinking if I jumped into it if I would go up to my knees or up to my waist." He was adamant that his facts were still accurate because it was indeed such a big event and "made a big impression." Asked whether he'll always remember it as he wrote it, Richard said, "I don't know about fifty years. I think they [journalists] stretched [the truth of] it like in the memoirs [stories from those who had been in the last blizzard in 1947]. I don't think [my own story] is stretched." Richard was certain that he told the absolute truth in his account. He was aware that years later someone might consider it a tad extreme, but he knew for a fact that what he wrote was what had happened.

Many of us have associations and memories tied to significant historical events. I vividly recall the intercom announcement in my sixth-grade classroom informing us that President John F. Kennedy had been shot. Also, hearing my parents speak of persecution under Hitler is different from reading about it in a book. Being in the Blizzard of '96 reminded my students and me that we were a part of the flow of history. My students' stories join the weather records, newspaper articles, television videos, and photographs as first-person accounts of a historical event.

Memoirs

Memoirs are a special form of personal history. They are emotional works, not journalistic or expository writings about the past. Memoir writers use the facts of their lives as raw material, to be molded and crafted into beautiful pieces of literature. Be it a poem, a short story, or an essay, the memoir is a work of art. In *Inventing the Truth* (1995), William Zinsser writes that "memoir assumes the life and ignores most of it. A memoir writer takes us back to a moment in his or her life that was unusually vivid, such as childhood, or that was framed by war or travel or some other exceptional event. By narrowing the lens the writer achieves a focus that's not possible in autobiography. Memoir is a window into a life" (p. 11).

For many years my final literature unit of the year was on memoirs. I presented it as the culmination of my students' year as authors, inviting them first to read memoirs by authors they knew and then to write their own. My focus had been literary, having my students explore the connections between real life and fiction. We could also look at how writers craft elements of their life into extraordinary pieces of writing. For example, Roald Dahl's memoir *Boy* is full of material that shows up in his books for children. James Thurber wrote about his family in hilarious ways. Paul Zindel, in *The Pigman and Me,* brought the art of memoir to a different and compelling level. Immersed in the art of memoir, my students were inspired to write their own. These we published, and soon I had a classroom collection of student memoirs to add to our professional writers' memoirs. Tonsillectomies, pets, family events, and travel were popular topics. While personal narrative was the most common genre, some children explored poetry and cartoon strips as vehicles for memoir writing as well.

As history came to the forefront of my teaching, my approach to the unit on memoir altered. It now became another way for us to consider history. Where did fact and fiction split? The children and I raised more questions of the texts we read. Where were these authors moving away from truth? Were their memoirs totally honest? I told them of the questions many had raised about Dahl's memoirs, and the thought that they might be as fanciful as his fiction. We began to look more closely at realistic fiction and wonder if some was based on the author's life. I had found previously that children could be tenacious about what they considered the truth. If they were writing a story about a trip to Florida, it started when they got up, and proceeded to their having breakfast and making the trip to the airport. All my efforts to convince them that it wasn't necessary to put in so many details if there was nothing special about them were for naught. It happened, so it had to be in the text, so many children thought. However, when we started considering memoirs in tandem with our history studies, children loosened up. Somehow, juxtaposed with history, they could more clearly see how memoirs could be works of art, based on the truth, but not locked into it.

One year one of my students wrote an amazing story about a skateboarding mishap. It sounded a bit dramatic, but the author insisted that it was the complete truth. Some years later he admitted that it was exaggerated. We had noted the way other authors expanded the truth and he had chosen to do that with his story; yet he didn't feel comfortable acknowledging it until sometime later. I was then able to use his skateboard story along with the information that it was "stretched" history with subsequent classes as we explored the interplay of personal history and memoir. Personal history became the landscape within which the children ranged—a field full of the facts, events, and emotions of their very own past.

The children selected books to read from a large collection of profession-ally published memoirs as well as memoirs from earlier classes. They read with great interest and responded to the memoirs in journals and in class discussions. I asked them to consider whether the books they were reading were based only on truth, and asked them to read favorite sections to the class. We explored how some authors wrote in short vignettes while others wrote novels based on aspects of their lives. In addition to their own reading, I read aloud: picture books such as Cynthia Rylant's *When I Was Young in the Mountains* and James Stevenson's *When I Was Nine;* essays such as James Thurber's "The Night the Bed Fell"; sections from Sandra Cisneros's *The House on Mango Street.*

Most interesting was the children's response to Christopher Paul Curtis's book, *The Watsons Go to Birmingham 1963,* which I read to them as part of a unit on civil rights. When I asked them why they thought I was reading the book to them they immediately said that it was because the book was a fic-tionalized memoir. I had expected them to answer that I was reading the book because it was about race, and I was surprised and delighted when they noted the autobiographical quality of the text, something I had not been conscious of at all.

The children discovered, as they wrote their own memoirs, that their options were limitless. They could start with the facts, but then manipulate them, alter them, and even eliminate them for the artistic whole. They didn't have to write about big events; little events, my young authors discovered, were often at the heart of the best memoirs. Ten-year-olds often feel that they haven't enough to write about, that they haven't lived long enough, done enough, had excitement enough. Writing memoirs invites them to recognize the power of their own lives—how much beauty exists in them waiting to be brought out in writing.

The memoirs unit proved to be a perfect way to tie together fact and fic-tion, history and literature. Highly personal, it was a way for my students to select what was most significant to them in their own histories and to be free to tell it any way they wished.

Richard's memoir was called "Stitches." Like several of my students, when I first introduced the unit Richard was stymied for a topic. Nothing in his life had sufficient drama, in his opinion, to be put down in writing. While some children were able to create long lists of topics, delighted to write about their previous years, others like Richard were more particular. "How about writing about a pet?" I'd say.

"No, that's too boring."

"Well then, how about your birthday party? I remember you telling me about it. It sounded like a lot of fun."

"No. We had cake. We played games. Nothing happened. That's boring."

"But you can play with it. Stretch the truth, if you want, to make it interesting. That is the luxury of a writer. Make it more fiction if you want."

"No. I want to write a true story. I want it to be history."

Such children were always my greatest challenge. Often sending them home to look at photo albums would do the trick. In Richard's case it was seeing the memoirs of other children that helped. I showed the class a variety of previously published student memoirs. The topics varied from trips to family events to accidents. The accidents were by far the most popular. Full of blood, broken bones, hospitals, and drama, these events seemed worthwhile personal history for many. Not boring!

The event that Richard chose to write about took place at the end of his third-grade year, he wrote about it at the end of fourth grade, and even six months later he was confident that he had told the story as truthfully as possible. While he felt that he might not remember it as well in twenty years, as a fifth grader he still felt that the facts were accurate. "Someone else might think that I was stretching it, but I wasn't." Richard wrote his memoir as a history and was careful to leave nothing out of the experience as he recalled it. The following excerpts from "Stitches" help to show how Richard worked as a historian in writing about this experience. Unlike other memoirists, Richard was not willing to play around with the experience. He wanted his account to ring as true as possible.

Richard was certain that the whole thing happened because of the apples. That is, if his mother hadn't spoken to their neighbors about the apple problem, the neighbor's kids wouldn't have asked Richard to play hockey and he wouldn't have gotten hurt. Suggesting that he start with the accident was futile. For Richard this story began with apples.

Getting Ready

Apples were getting thrown into our backyard from the house behind us, so my mom and I went over to tell the people behind us that neighborhood kids were throwing apples into our backyard.

Their mother said that they really tried to pick up all the apples on the ground, but they never could.

My mom and I started to go back home when one of the neighbor's sons came running out to ask us if my brothers and I wanted to play hockey and I said yes.

After I got my brothers to come, I had to put my rollerblades on. When we got there, we broke up into teams.

Playing

After we were playing for a while and I was in goal, one of the neighbor's sons was coming at me with the puck. He shot and it hit my forehead. (Sorry, I forgot to tell you I was not wearing a helmet.)

Blood

I put my hand up to my head. It hurt really badly. All that time my mom was just sitting there thinking I was okay but after I took my hand off my head and it was drenched in blood, my brothers saw and skated over to tell her.

Richard was not above the slight exaggeration for dramatic effect. He achieved drama mostly through his illustrations; however, he was proud of how he had used his words to exaggerate the situation in the above excerpt. "I read *Boy*," he said. Dahl "said that his nose was hanging on a string [after a car crash]. So I said that my hand was covered in blood, but it wasn't. Some blood, but not 'drenched.'"

Going to the Hospital

It took five minutes to go to the hospital because it was a Saturday and very few people were on the road.

When we got to the hospital we were looking for a parking space but all the empty spots said RESERVED FOR DOCTORS ONLY.

We finally parked and walked into the Emergency Room. When we checked in at the desk we had to wait five minutes until someone called us.

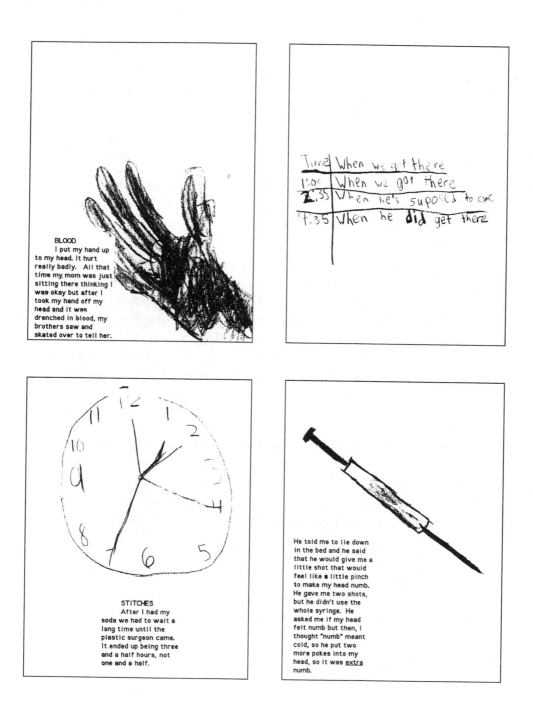

BLOOD
I put my hand up to my head. It hurt really badly. All that time my mom was just sitting there thinking I was okay but after I took my hand off my head and it was drenched in blood, my brothers saw and skated over to tell her.

Time	When we got there
1:00	When we got there
2:35	When he's suposed to come
4:35	When he did get there

STITCHES
After I had my soda we had to wait a long time until the plastic surgeon came. It ended up being three and a half hours, not one and a half.

He told me to lie down in the bed and he said that he would give me a little shot that would feel like a little pinch to make my head numb. He gave me two shots, but he didn't use the whole syringe. He asked me if my head felt numb but then, I thought "numb" meant cold, so he put two more pokes into my head, so it was <u>extra</u> numb.

At the Hospital

The doctor on duty looked at the cut and said that it would be better to get a plastic surgeon to stitch up the cut. That meant that we would have to wait one and a half hours for the plastic surgeon to arrive.

Stitches

After I had my soda we had to wait a long time until the plastic surgeon came. It ended up being three and a half hours, not one and a half.

The plastic surgeon had the loudest shirt in the world. It was orange, with different colored flowers all over it.

The above excerpts show what Richard remembers most of all about the experience. How long everything took! The pain seemed less significant than all the waiting. Time looms large in this story. Not only did Richard insist on the accurate chronology of the event (even including the seemingly irrelevant apples of the beginning), but he vividly recollected the long wait at the hospital for the plastic surgeon. It is hard to miss the ironic quality of the five minutes it took to get to the hospital versus the hours they waited for the plastic surgeon.

Safety

So, from now on, my mom makes me wear a helmet whenever I play hockey even if it is with a ball.

Richard took his position as historian very seriously. It was important that everything he remembered be included in his story. He was willing to be creative only if it was part of the story. The plastic surgeon's colorful shirt was amusing, but true as well. The most Richard was willing to do to "stretch the truth" was to exaggerate the amount of blood at the time of the accident. For Richard, sticking to the facts of the story was important. Whereas other memoirists may be willing to play around with the information in order to add drama and beauty to their writing, Richard was uncompromising in his belief that the story has to be written down as it had happened.

Reflecting Back

When I reflect on the meaning of personal history activities, three ideas stand out. The first is *the importance of our own stories*. As historians, we all try to make sense of our past, how personal events have affected others, how major events have affected us. Through memoir writing, children can learn that their own stories matter and can be viewed through the eyes of a historian just as other people's histories are.

Another lesson I learned was *the importance of grabbing the moment.* I realized with the Blizzard of '96 that it was important to be on the lookout for potentially significant historical events that my students could consider themselves part of. The following school year the Yankees won the World Series, and my colleagues and I took advantage of that historical moment to explore ways of documenting history. One colleague showed his students how to record the score, and he and another colleague debated before their two classes the advantages and disadvantages of numerical data over verbal data. I asked my students to write about their own memories of the Series for posterity. Some produced pages of scores while others preferred to focus on their own emotional response to the World Series. Even those who lacked interest in sports were caught up in the excitement and wrote of that. The Blizzard and the World Series were two events that are now part of New York City's history. The unique opportunities each presented to bring history to our doorstep made me realize that I must always be flexible and ready when the next such moment comes along.

Finally, I learned the value and place of *stretching the truth.* Memoirs had long been a part of my writing program. Thinking about them in the context of teaching and learning history was new. It made me more alert to the way truth is often a part of fiction and led me to bring history more into my literature discussions with children.

■ ■ ■

On the last page of Richard's portfolio is his fourth grade's final class song with a note he wrote: "This is the last thing we're going to do this year."

From "Rock Around Dalton"

Fourth Graders are number one,
We go to school and have lots of fun.
We learn a lot every day,
because that's the Dalton way.
We can't wait to start fifth grade!

The fourth graders sang their song at the school's closing assembly with confidence and gusto. No longer newcomers to the building, they belonged and were ready to move on to the next year. Richard moved on too, to fifth grade, with fourth grade now part of his personal history.

 # Zooming In

Memory

In a piece in the *New York Times Book Review,* author Anna Quindlen notes that she will never be a memoir writer because she has a lousy memory. She is skeptical about the memories of others, wondering how writers can recall events that occurred more than thirty years ago. True to her journalist's training, she is more comfortable with those memoirists who rely on "the wisdom of distance, hindsight, and secondary source material." When contemplating her own sources, she believes she has little to draw on. Her childhood diaries don't yield much. Her high school journal is "largely a recitation of trips to the Villager shop in Princeton; perhaps I was shallow, perhaps only young" (p. 35).

Memory, Quindlen reminds us, is very much shaped by stories retold, photographs, and other memorabilia; "only the most able and most honest memoirist can make the distinction between these cumulatively constructed tableaux and what really happened." She contends, "Fact is different from truth, and truth is different from insight" (p. 35). Writing about the night of her mother's death, she wonders if it was as cold as she remembers. She is driven to verify the actual temperature, to reassure herself that the temperature was in fact as cold as she describes. The detail sets the stage for her description of her feelings. But a larger question remains: does it really matter to anyone but herself? Would the readers of her memoirs wonder if she remembered it accurately or not? Would they even care? Perhaps, in the end, she is correct: she could never write her memoirs, because she is overly concerned about the accuracy of her own memories. This is an issue all memoir writers must address: would all of the participants in a story described in a memoir agree about what actually happened?

What, then, to make of the ephemeral nature of memory? How does one decide what is important and what is not? Is it what was most significant to the individual? What about what was most important to the family as a group?

The question of the nature of memory is closely linked to the issue of the role of memory in the construction of historical knowledge. Issues of what students should learn are related to what should be memorized. In the past, educators believed that in order to attain historical understanding, students had to acquire historical knowledge through memorizing a vast corpus of facts. Today, many educators believe that memorizing is antithetical to process, inquiry, and constructivist theories of learning. Other theorists are not so sure that memorization should be abandoned entirely.

Kieran Egan believes that memorization is underutilized, that it is important for the development of imaginative thinking. "One of the clear implications of the consistent observation of the relationship between memory and imagination," he writes, "is the importance of memorizing knowledge, facts, chunks of prose and poetry, formulae, etc. for the stimulation and development of the imagination. Ignorance, in short, starves the imagination . . . Only knowledge in our memories is accessible to the action of imagination. We can only construct possible worlds, can only think of things as possibly being so, out of what we already know" (1992, p. 52). Egan doesn't address the erratic nature of memory retrieval, but asks educators to attend more to the importance of knowledge acquisition to ensure that students have information in their memory that will stimulate imaginative thinking.

In *A Workshop of the Possible: Nurturing Children's Creative Development,* Ruth Shagoury Hubbard also argues for greater attention to memory as a learning tool for children. She believes that teachers have relegated memory to "a cobwebbed storage vault, with certain items being stored in 'long-term' memory and others waiting in the wings, ready to be spit out of 'short-term' memory onto tests and into oblivion. It's time we take a fresh look at the role of memory, in learning and making meaning. It is an important invisible tool for children as they hone their creative minds" (p. 83). Hubbard reviews recent developments in memory research and writes compellingly of the processing theory articulated by researchers such as Craik and Lockhart (1972). "The cornerstone of the processing theory," writes Hubbard, "is that we have some control over how we think about information in our environment—especially how deeply we choose to think about it" (p. 88). Shallow processing is superficial, nonmeaningful learning of, for example, state capitals for a test, while deep processing is the sort of knowledge that one wants to remember—knowledge that is meaningful to the individual. Methods to encourage deep processing, to make memory retrieval personally important, argues Hubbard, need to be made much more central to teaching.

Egan and Hubbard encourage greater reflection about the importance of memory in teaching and learning. Memories are constantly altering, they dim as one forgets, they become richer as new knowledge is learned and older theories are reworked. Students can think critically about memory just as they do about other aspects of learning. Whether writing personal memoirs or considering the memoirs of historical figures, students can be encouraged to think about the role of memory. "Memory is a construction, not an imprint," wrote George Johnson in a *New York Times* article on evolving theories on memory. "In trying to dredge up the past, we grasp at scraps of evidence fluttering inside our heads" (p. 10).

 # Booktalk

Inventing the Truth: The Art and Craft of Memoir
edited by William Zinsser

Ever wonder how well-known writers approach the writing of a memoir? William Zinsser, writer and editor, has compiled an excellent collection of essays that address the question. Using transcripts of the talks given by eight writers at the New York Public Library in 1986, Zinsser has captured the flavor of how each individual approaches writing about his or her life. In his 1995 revision of the book, Zinsser selected four new writers to add to the original group. By interviewing them himself and then editing the interviews to delete his questions, he has expanded the scope of the original book to include issues of writing about painful memories (Eileen Simpson), of the importance of family mementos and papers as a trigger for memory (Ian Frazier), of the development of an authentic voice reflecting a minority culture (Henry Louis Gates, Jr.), and of creating a new life in a distant land (Jill Ker Conway). Along with the original essays by Russell Baker, Alfred Kazin, Annie Dillard, and Toni Morrison, Zinsser's collection can serve as powerful inspiration for memoir writing. Although the book has found a wide audience among teachers of high school and college students, it is of interest to teachers of younger grades as well. The message of both the individual essays and the book as a whole is to be true to your own experience. What better message to convey to a beginning writer of any age? The book also contains a useful bibliographic essay, in which each writer comments on the memoirs that influenced him or her.

Material World: A Global Family Portrait
by Peter Menzel

What if families were asked to pose for a picture with most of their possessions displayed? What would those portraits tell us about the lives of the people?

How would you, as a viewer, interpret the resulting images of families from many different countries? These are exactly the kinds of questions *Material World,* an unusual photographic and statistical portrait of families, seeks to answer in a novel approach to looking at the life of the rich and the poor. Sixteen photographers traveled around the world in 1994 and spent a week living with an average family in thirty different countries. The photographers took large-format portraits of the families gathered with most of their possessions outside of their house. Close-ups capture elements of daily life for each family. Certain items not photographed, such as built-in furniture and other unmovable objects, trees, and some animals, are cataloged at the end of the book. (In addition to creating a large portrait, the photographers shot video of the families as well, which have been incorporated into a CD-ROM that can be purchased separately from the book.)

Use this book to stimulate discussions about the importance of objects, about cultural values, about photographic point of view. Consider whether these images bring us closer to the people we see. Ask your students to generate questions they would like to ask the people in the book. Try to ascertain the emotions revealed in the photographs. Discuss the emotions the photos evoke in the viewer.

 ## Tools of the Trade

Family Photographs

Family photographs can be incorporated as another kind of historical evidence in a unit on personal history. Family photographs depict details of the past and so can serve as a trigger for memories, a place to begin memoir writing. Photographs also suggest the point of view of the photographer and what was valued by both the photographer and the audience.

It is important to remind students that just as a historian or memoirist selects data to create a coherent story, so does a photographer. A photographer is always making choices—sometimes intentionally, sometimes unintentionally—deciding what will be within the frame and what will be just beyond. The composition of the image is only part of the shaping of a point of view. A photographer, or others who compile the images, can also add meaning by sequencing images or using text to influence the interpretation of the viewer. Even a label in a family album imposes meaning on an image. A witty caption, a date, or a description of the event can shed light either on the photographer's intention or the compiler's interpretation of the image.

In working with students' personal histories there may be a wide range of photographic images available: casual color snapshots that capture recent family events, formal black-and-white portraits of older relatives, hand-tinted images of family ancestors, or the children's own photographs of family members. By selecting images from a family's collection, a student is imposing another level of meaning. This point should be made explicit to the students as you remind them again of the selective nature of historical analysis. A single image of an individual can contain the makings of an entire story. The interpretation of the image is shaped by the relationship between the subject and the viewer.

When you think about using photographs, consider incorporating their use into other historical units to broaden the range of evidence students examine. Images of environments you are reading about and old photographs of ceremonies or historic events all add a new dimension to the analysis. Although there is a wide range of photographic compilations available in book form, be creative in your search for images. Check with your local museum or historical society to see what reproductions can be purchased from them. Ask children to bring in photographs relating to a particular topic. A child's photograph of his grandfather's store on the Lower East Side was an excellent addition to one class's study of immigration to New York. Look for images that may be available on-line, such as the collections available from the American Memory site mentioned in Chapter 1.

There are many ways to approach the analysis of images to enhance the study of history. Photographs can be copied for class discussion, so that the images can be handled by the whole group. Students can record their observations of a single photograph individually or work in small groups to share observations about a series of images. Another option is to convert a few images into slides that can be projected for a class discussion. By enlarging images, students may be able to notice details more easily. Have students look at small parts of a detailed scene and make observations about each section. Discuss what lies within the scene, what might be just beyond.

Students can begin to use images by examining either an individual photograph or a series and writing down details of what they observe. They can base their statements on what they already know about the subject. Photographs can be used to elicit questions about the topic and can be a starting point for research.

Once students have used photographs as historic documents, there are many ways to extend their use. Students can use them to spark imaginative writing about individuals or events. Students in a class can also create their own photographs as documents about a historical topic. A class trip to a neighborhood or a historic site can be an opportunity to create a photographic essay. By dividing the class into small groups that share the responsibility for collecting visual evidence, the class can construct both a record of their individual points of view about an experience and a collective remembrance. It is always interesting to see the range of images captured by different groups. And what better way for students to understand the selective nature of the photographic record than to have them create their own.

Personal Artifacts

We all have personal objects or artifacts that are special to us, that evoke memories and feelings. Just as family photographs can be used as a form of historical evidence, so can the objects that are an integral part of family life.

For an article in the *New York Times,* photographer Georgia Scott traveled to shelters for the homeless and a hospital to see what kinds of personal possessions held special meaning for people in dire circumstances. Some of the objects are expected—a Bible, jewelry, a watch, photographs of family members. Some objects, however, are more startling—a book of love poems given as a gift by a prison guard, a desk appearance ticket that reminds someone of a center where they used to live and gives them hope to enter a rehabilitation program, a wallet given by a former girlfriend that provides inspiration to change, or a toy merry-go-round that reminds a young adult of happier times. Although the article provides only brief quotes from each individual, the objects shown could have been used by the owners as a focus for writing personal history.

To incorporate personal objects as a stimulus to writing history, you need to give some thought as to the kinds of objects you want students to select. In writing about their own life, children may initially think about comfort objects such as favorite dolls, toys, or souvenirs. While these objects may be great as a stimulus for memoir writing, try to encourage them to consider a broader range of objects. A favorite book, a letter from a teacher, a sports trophy, a shell from the beach, an object found on a walk in the park can also be stimulating. When they are considering writing about their relationships with other members of the family, encourage them to think carefully about the individual. A tool used by a parent, a bottle of cologne, a treasured keepsake passed on from a great-grandparent, a trophy won by an older sibling are the kinds of objects that can be useful. The more experience children have analyzing objects, the more likely they are to broaden their view as to what they might choose.

Researching On-Line

As you contemplate creating assignments for writing memoirs and personal history, you might consider how your students' doing an on-line search might change the experience. By accessing on-line publications, maps, or news articles, students can create another kind of reference for writing personal history. They can check facts about an event or see what was happening in their community on a particular day.

Doing this kind of research presents its own challenges. Beginning a computer search of a topic involves defining the topic with keywords that are narrow enough to yield meaningful results and selecting an appropriate search engine. Depending on the search engine selected, there are different ways to proceed. Two types of searching—Gopher, which is text-based, and the World Wide Web, which incorporates visual and sound information—can be experimented with. The Web is a newer way to connect to various locations. To access the Web, you need a browsing program, such as Netscape or Internet Explorer. You then select a search engine, which maintains a list or index of the Web pages it can access. When a user enters a request, or query, the search engine reviews its catalog to locate pages that contain the requested phrase. The user is then shown a list of the sites the search engine has found. It is important to remember that there are frequent changes on the Web, however; sites that are available now may not be available later. Also, it is not unusual to try links recommended on one site only to discover that the recommended site is no longer available. Web addresses may also change, and while a pointer may be used to direct you to a new address, pointers are not always provided.

Search engines differ in the way their lists are created. With what is called an *active search engine,* such as AltaVista, HotBot, Lycos, InfoSeek Ultra, or WebCrawler, to name a few, the search engine creates the list. In a *passive search engine,* such as Yahoo, individuals or institutions list their Web pages with the search engine. A *meta-search engine,* such as MetaCrawler or Internet Sleuth, uses the catalogs of other engines by forwarding a query to them and then listing the results. A service such as Netscape's Net Search allows a user to access several catalogs or lists from a single page, but one at a time. Depending on which kind of search engine you select, you will get different results. Often one search engine will find pages that others don't.

To search effectively, you need to develop a strategy. Although active search engines may locate a specific location more quickly, a passive search engine may be better for locating general resources or the main page of a particular Web site. You should try different search engines, and be persistent. The success of a search depends on the ability to use the features of a particular search tool.

There are excellent on-line references that can help decipher the way search engines work. On of the most thorough and useful sites has been prepared by the University of California, Berkeley, Library. The pages provide an overview of search tools, specific strategies to help you define a topic, a discussion of how to select a search tool, as well as instructions for constructing searches for various search engines.

When conducting searches it is generally recommended that bookmarks (sometimes referred to by other terms, such as "favorites" or "hotlinks") be used to remember your favorite sites and to allow you to access them more quickly in the future. If you spend the time to learn how to organize the sites you've located using bookmarks, returning to the sites will be much simpler.

Once you have used search engines to locate sites, it is essential that you critically evaluate the sites for content. Many excellent references are available to help educators learn how to evaluate sites. For on-line references for evaluation, see Esther Grassian's *Thinking Critically About World Wide Web Resources* (1995) and the evaluation tools and bibliography available on-line from Cornell University and Widener University (address given below).

If your school is not yet hard-wired to allow you to access the World Wide Web from school, commercial services that you can subscribe to from home also provide access to the Web.

For additional information about using search engines, refer to articles published by EdWeb (address below).

The following are addresses for the Web sites and search engines cited in this section, as well as other useful sites:

University of California Library Web:
http://www.lib.berkeley.edu/TeachingLib/Guides/Internet
AltaVista: http://www.altavista.digital.com/
Lycos: http://www.lycos.com/
WebCrawler: http://www.webcrawler.com/

Yahoo: http://www.yahoo.com/

HotBot: http://www.hotbot.com/

InfoSeek Ultra: http://ultra.infoseek.com/

MetaCrawler: http://www.metacrawler.com/

Internet Sleuth: http://www.isleuth.com/

Netscape Net Search: when in Netscape, press the Net Search button *or*
   http://www.netscape.com/

Microsoft Internet Explorer: http://www.microsoft.com/ie/

EdWeb: http://edweb.gsn.org/resource.cntnts.html

Esther Grassian's article:
   http://www.library.ucla.edu/libraries/college/instruct/critical.htm

Cornell University web evaluation criteria and tools:
   http://www.library.cornell.edu/okuref/research/webeval.html

Widener University tools and bibliography:
   http://www.science.widener.edu/~withers/evalout.htm *and*
   http://www.science.widener.edu/~withers/wbstrbib.htm

CHAPTER THREE

Other People's Stories:
Immigration

"It felt good to become a citizen!" As Elizabeth read the final words of her story I held her book up high so that the audience could see the accompanying artwork. Even as I did, I worked to regain my composure, wondering what I could possibly say after that last story, an extraordinary chronicle of a Holocaust survivor. It was December, and we were in the high school library, a spacious room well lit by enormous windows. Books and computers mingle with plants, tables, and comfortable chairs. This was our class's Immigrant Oral History Celebration, and the children had just finished presenting their picture books, histories they had constructed from interviews they had conducted. I looked around at my students, their parents, and the many interviewees present. It had been a moving experience, listening to these stories being read with the protagonists at hand.

While I was familiar with all the stories, having worked with my students on them for weeks, they became something new and different read aloud in the library. Now I watched Ariel's grandfather as he listened to her reading about his immigration from Hungary. Emma's doorman sat up ramrod straight, intently listening to her interpretation of his journey from Moldova. As Elana read her baby-sitter's harsh story, many listeners' eyes filled with tears. These may have been ordinary people, but their stories were hardly simple. I thought about the remarkable hardships these immigrants had experienced: losing family through the Holocaust, facing starvation while fleeing through a rain forest in Asia, coming to a strange land while leaving one's children behind. Somehow, my students had captured a quality to these histories that made the immigrant experience fresh for me, a first-generation American.

Finally, I knew what to say. "I want to thank everyone here today for being part of this celebration. It is a celebration of immigration, especially the immigration of all our subjects today. It is also a celebration of our young historians who have worked hard and carefully to capture each immigrant's particular history of his or her journey to America."

Dalton School fourth graders are newcomers to our building, having immigrated from an intimate primary school to a busy, teeming upper school. From a cozy five-story townhouse to a vast twelve-story building, it is quite a change. No longer do they enter a soft, carpeted lobby full of kindly parents, familiar teachers, and smaller children. Now they walk into an enormous, impersonal lobby full of unruly teenagers rushing to get to the elevators, shoving aside the smaller newcomers as they go. Once in the elevators, the fourth graders are squashed by big people with big packs, and woe be it to the child that complains! It is only when the elevator doors finally open to the ninth floor that our new fourth graders can enter and begin to relax in a space that is truly theirs. Who has not had a similar experience at some point in life? I completed sixth grade in a small elementary school and was completely overwhelmed by the large junior high I went to next.

To help with this difficult transition, the Dalton social studies curriculum begins with a study of immigration: fourth graders to the middle school and others to the United States. First-generation American myself, I identify strongly with my students' desires and difficulties as they work to assimilate into the middle school and learn about U.S. immigration. Personal history, New York City, my colleagues, available resources, and my students all strongly influence the direction I take with this unit.

I am the daughter of German Jews; most of my family was forced to immigrate to the United States, Israel, England, and Brazil because of Hitler. Still, we maintain close ties to Germany. Many of our closest family friends still live there, as well as some relatives who returned or were overlooked during the war. Due to my father's academic career (he is a specialist in German politics), we moved a great deal. I attended a variety of schools in Germany and in Midwestern towns where there were no other families like ours. In fourth grade, I remember begging my parents to send me to Sunday School so that I could be like all my friends. There were no local synagogues; my parents found some Jewish graduate students who provided religious classes at their home. Being the only American in a German country school or the only child with parents who spoke with an accent in a homogeneous American school, I grew up knowing firsthand about the difficulties of assimilation.

In my earlier days as a fourth-grade teacher of U.S. history I did as my colleagues did: based my teaching on the textbook scope and sequence, adding on creative projects. Since none of my colleagues took field trips, I didn't either. However, when thinking anew about teaching immigration I knew that I wanted New York City to be an important aspect of our studies. My main difficulty was in choosing what part of the city: Ellis Island, the Statue of Liberty, the Lower East Side, Little Italy, El Museo del Barrio, the Tenement Museum, and the Chinatown Historical Society were only a few of the many possibilities. Even walking half a block away from the school to Lexington Avenue and turning the corner gave me a wealth of possibilities. There was the Indian news dealer next to the Korean market, just a few doors away from the Chinese restaurant, and only blocks away from a Russian fast food place, an old German bakery, and a Mexican take-out shop.

Several colleagues had already developed and taught rich immigration units for several years, and I looked to them for ideas as I planned my own unit. Two of them centered their units around family history. I had always greatly admired the results of these studies: beautifully published books of family immigration stories, family tree posters, maps tracking each family's journey to America, and other artifacts of individual family history. It seemed an excellent way for me to achieve many of my teaching goals. Family history was intimate. Children became historians, and constructing projects out of such highly personal data helped to make history real and meaningful to them. Additionally, the projects clearly emphasized the diversity inherent in the immigrant experience. Finally, the projects inspired creativity, and the children clearly were proud of them. However, I worried that there might be children and families for whom such projects were difficult. I knew it would have been very disturbing for my parents to help me with such a research project in fourth grade, especially having to explain about my grandfather, who died in a concentration camp. I recalled my friend's seventh-grade daughter, who was assigned to do a biography of a grandparent. Since her surviving grandparents were Holocaust survivors unable to discuss their past, my friend had to go to the school and explain the situation to the teacher on behalf of her very shy daughter. (Of course, once the teacher was alerted to the problem a variation of the assignment was arranged.) Then there were the nontraditional situations I had come across over the years: adopted children, lesbian and gay families, single parents who refused to discuss the other parent, grandparents raising grandchildren, and those who could only trace their history back one generation. I wanted to be sure that any project I designed was inviting and comfortable for all.

When seeking out resources on immigration for elementary children, I found that most materials focused on the great wave of American immigration at the beginning of the twentieth century. Ellis Island and the Statue of Liberty were symbols of this time; the grainy images of poor Eastern European peasants crowding through the Ellis Island entrance hall or pouring into the streets of New York's Lower East Side had become the quintessential image of American immigration. However, all American immigrants did not come through Ellis Island or from Europe, and not all came at the same time. Mexicans came by foot across our southern border, Chinese first arrived by boat from across the Pacific to build the railroads, and still arrive today, often to work in Chinese restaurants, in laundries, and in sweatshops in the garment industry. Whereas many of those who went through Ellis Island came to this country seeking economic opportunity, many others came to escape war. For example, many Southeast Asians immigrated after the Vietnam War. Then there are the immigrants of today who surround my upper-middle-class students: baby-sitters, doormen, and taxi drivers, most likely recent immigrants from the Caribbean and Latin America. Much as I appreciated the idea of Ellis Island, Lewis Hines's photographs of immigrants, the many picture books and chapter books for children on the massive waves of European immigration, I wanted my students to connect to more recent immigration, to interact with living immigrants, not only those from eighty years ago. The politics of immigration have become intense: often those who came to this country earlier no longer want others to come. I wanted my students to gain some sense of these controversies, to approach immigration in the recent past rather than the far past.

During the summer of 1995, I spent a great deal of time thinking about immigration. I visited many traditional historical sites and museums. I read about immigration, family history, oral history. The unit I finally put together focused on three areas:

- *Being an immigrant:* The children's own experience as immigrants to a new school building.
- *Immigration immersion:* Becoming knowledgeable about American immigration through mini-projects, reading books, taking field trips, and other activities.
- *Being an oral historian:* Reconstructing an immigrant's experience through an oral history book project. Children could choose to interview a relative, a friend, anyone they wished.

My Goals

My goals for the immigration unit were several in number:

- By considering immigration in different ways and working on an oral history project I hoped that my students' definition of history would deepen and broaden.
- My students would create history: they would interview immigrants about their journeys and construct these interviews into historical narratives. In other words, they would become historians.
- My hope was that the children would be able to generalize their own journey to a new school to the experiences of actual immigrants to America. At the same time, I hoped that they would recognize that their experiences were not as profound as an actual immigrant's.

- The oral history project was designed to make the recent past become immediate and real. Many of the immigrants' reasons for making the move related to larger historical events such as wars.
- I wanted my students to understand immigration. I wanted it to feel real. I didn't want it to seem far away and distant to them. Immigration has built America; it is our past, present, and future. I wanted my students to understand its importance.
- The children's own experiences and those of the immigrants they would encounter through books, trips, and interviews would increase their knowledge of the immigrant experience and thus help them to become more empathetic, ethical, and moral. I was particularly hopeful that they would be able to better empathize with those immigrants whose experiences were very different from their own families, especially recent immigrants.
- Connecting different immigrant experiences I hoped would help the children see how the past affects the present and the future. My students could see how past immigration affected New York City and how it does so today. During the 1996–97 school year we also noted the attention paid to immigration in politics.

Being an Immigrant

On the first day of school our very nervous, very new fourth graders fill out "citizenship applications." After presenting documentation such as health forms and the required school supplies, each child receives an "alien registration card," the all-important "green card" that starts them on the road to Big Dalton Citizenship. Within the first few days of school, we talk a great deal about citizenship. How does it differ from legal residency? What are the rights of American citizens? of Dalton citizens? What does it mean to be a good citizen of a place, a school, a country? While most of my students are American citizens, often other family members are originally from elsewhere. David's mother came from Israel with her whole family. Bobby's grandmother is from Morocco. Nathaniel's parents are French, while he is both French and American. To complicate his home life, he has a British nanny. New York City is teeming with immigrants, old and new. My students meet them as family friends, baby-sitters, doormen, taxi drivers, news sellers, teachers, waitresses, and candy store owners. Many of them come to fourth grade knowing a lot about the intricacies of citizenship, what a green card is, a sponsor. Immigrants are very real to my urban students.

In considering what it is like to be an immigrant, my students look at their own experience first. They draw pictures that illustrate their trip over from Little Dalton (the "old country"), complete with Park Avenue as a teeming, dangerous body of water, with their old school looking tiny and welcoming and the new school looking enormous and scary with crowds of big, disinterested high schoolers. We create a Museum of the Old Country, full of cherished artifacts from their primary school years. Elana contributed a picture book she had created in third grade, Alie offered a ceramic sculpture, Jesse brought in a class picture from kindergarten. To prepare for Big Dalton Citizenship they learn all they can about their new school. Every class takes on one aspect of the school to research and write about for a fourth-grade handbook. For several years my class did a Who's Who of Big Dalton, for which they interviewed a range of significant people from the headmaster to the school secretaries. More recently we have taken to mapping the building. Finally, in January the entire fourth grade takes a citizenship test based on their handbook work and is given certificates of Big Dalton Citizenship by the headmaster in a moving ceremony.

Immigration Immersion

I begin my unit on immigration with a variety of activities and experiences designed to deepen my students' knowledge of immigration. During the 1996–97 school year immigration was in the news a lot. My students and I searched the newspapers for articles, brought them to school, and discussed them. At one point, New York City's Mayor Giuliani decided to be a spokesperson on behalf of immigrants. A colleague had her class write the mayor on immigration, and in response he sent a representative who spoke to the whole fourth grade about immigration issues in New York today. I read aloud certain books, such as Margy Brun Knight's *Who Belongs Here?* and Bette Bao Lord's *In the Year of the Boar and Jackie Robinson.* Since so many of my students were of European descent I wanted them to know of immigrants from other places. Knight's book is about a young Cambodian war refugee, a composite of the many she has taught over the years. Bette Bao Lord's book is a fictionalized account of her childhood immigration to the United States from China.

In small groups the children researched and created posters that illustrated contributions to American English from Native Americans, African Americans, European Americans, Asian Americans, and Hispanic Americans. We took trips to Ellis Island and the Tenement Museum and watched videos that gave us more information about turn-of-the-century immigration. I even showed Charlie Chaplin's silent short *The Immigrant.* Chaplin, an immigrant himself, makes fun of the stereotype of the poor European immigrant.

In keeping with our role as historians I had my students take a walking tour of lower Manhattan, documenting through photography the cultural diversity brought about by immigration. The children were divided into small groups with at least one adult for each group, and they planned their tour the day before. I provided them with a map and a list of possible places to go. The maps I gave included the Lower East Side (which had been a predominantly Eastern European Jewish area), Chinatown, and Little Italy. The trip was a great success. My group had a wonderful time looking for ways Chinatown was filtering into a formerly Jewish neighborhood. They found an old Polish bank that had been turned into a Chinese enterprise, a Buddhist temple, an old synagogue, and a church. As for stores, they found exotic (to them) Chinese tea and herbal stores, Gus's Pickles, an old Jewish candy shop, and a Chinese ice cream parlor. The next day in school, each group assembled their photos on a piece of oak tag and wrote captions for them to create a historical document of their tour.

Being an Oral Historian

The idea of having fourth graders do oral histories is one I picked up from a former fourth-grade colleague who had her students interview Dalton alumni for our fourth-grade handbook. In fact, if I hadn't seen my colleague's students conduct interviews, manage tape recorders, and transcribe so well, I'm sure I would never have considered doing oral histories with my own class.

When I began planning this unit I knew that oral histories of immigrants would be a major part of it. The idea of using picture books came about when I discovered *I Was Dreaming to Come to America* (Lawlor 1995), a beautifully illustrated book of excerpts from the Ellis Island Oral History Project. Soon I was searching out everything I could about oral histories. I mentioned my interest to Stephanie. To my great delight she told me that she was an experienced oral historian and would be happy to help with the project.

Stephanie and I decided to begin by modeling the process for the children. We would discuss what oral history was, help the children create good interview questions, model an interview for them, demonstrate how to extract significant quotes from a transcription, and show how to construct a compelling historical narrative from the quotes.

Introducing Oral History

Stephanie began with a lesson on the kinds of evidence that historians consider. Documents and artifacts led the list that the children offered of things that historians consider. The children easily distinguished primary and secondary sources, noting that diaries, journals, and first-person accounts typified the former, while CD-ROM encyclopedias, trade books, and almanacs were examples of the latter. Stephanie then had the children consider more closely the issue of primary sources and how we determine their truthfulness. Finally, she focused on oral history as a form of primary source data, one that we would be using to learn more about immigration to America.

Creating Interview Questions

At a subsequent class meeting, Stephanie helped the children generate a list of questions for the actual interviews. She encouraged them to think hard about the nature of good questions. How useful in an oral history interview would be a question that could be answered by yes or no? How narrow should a question be? What kind of response would an open-ended question evoke? What constituted a good follow-up question? The children came up with an excellent series of questions, which Stephanie wrote on chart paper. Then, with the children's help, she arranged the questions in an order that made sense. By the next day she had typed them up and made copies for all the children to use during the model interview and to guide them as they prepared for their own interviews.

Oral History Questions

1. Why did you emigrate?
2. Where did you come from, and where did you go when you first arrived?
3. When did you come here?
4. Who came with you?
5. How did you get to America? Tell me about some of your experiences.
6. How long was your trip? Tell me about it.
7. What did you think America would be like? What was it actually like?
8. Tell about your family at the time of your emigration.
9. Did anyone who came with you speak English? Did you? How did you learn English?
10. What was your childhood like?
11. What things did you bring with you? What was your most valued item, and did you bring it? Did you have to leave special things behind?

12. What was your lifestyle when you first came here?
13. Compare something from your old country with something in this country.
14. What were your feelings when you left?
15. How did you feel when you first came here?
16. What did you miss from the country you came from?
17. What did you like about your new country? What did you dislike?
18. Did you meet people when you first came here? Are you still friends with any of them?
19. What was the first landmark you saw? Do you have any stories about it?
20. What year did you become a citizen? When and where?
21. What did you need to know to become a citizen?
22. What was it like to become a citizen?

Finding a Person to Interview

We talked a lot about how to find an interview subject. The children discussed the immigrants they knew and whether they would be willing to be interviewed for such a project. For most, this was no problem. There were babysitters, grandparents, parents, family friends, teachers, and acquaintances.

Stephanie and I too thought about who should be our subject for the model interview. For the first year Stephanie asked a colleague who had immigrated from Panama to the United States at age nine. She was delighted to do the interview and brought a fascinating collection of family artifacts to share with the children both during and after the interview. The following year Stephanie interviewed my father, who had immigrated to the United States from Germany in 1936. He too greatly enjoyed the experience.

The Model Interview

At each session, Stephanie showed the children how to operate a tape recorder, how to check the sound, and how to turn it on and off during the interview. Each of the model interviews lasted around an hour. The children observed with remarkable concentration, fascinated by the subject's lives and the interview process itself. When Stephanie was finished the children added their own questions, which filled in some of the gaps regarding the subject's journey. After the first year's interview Stephanie transcribed it and returned to my class the next day able to show my students the strengths and weaknesses of the actual interview. In some cases she felt that she had not asked good follow-up questions or allowed enough time for answers to certain questions. In other cases she had allowed the subject to wander far from the topic at hand.

Stephanie commented on how tricky it was to keep the conversation going, listen carefully, and be sure that all the important topics were covered at the same time. Her ability to be self-critical amazed my students. One finally blurted out, "Don't be so hard on yourself!"

Extracting Significant Quotes from the Transcription

After my father's interview I transcribed most of the tape and then analyzed the transcription with my students. I didn't transcribe the whole tape because although some of my father's stories were wonderful, they were not about his immigration. Since the book I was working on was about my father's immigration, I explained to my students that I had decided not to transcribe these other stories, which saved me quite a bit of time. Together we looked for quotes that best told my father's immigration story. I showed the children how we could cut out extraneous parts and repetitions, demonstrating that not every word had to go into the final book. Finally, I showed them how to add missing information in brackets when necessary. Several boys were especially fascinated by this, saying that this was something they had noticed in newspaper interviews of their favorite sports figures.

Creating a Prototype Picture Book

For my father's interview, we did a prototype picture book. Each child selected one quote to illustrate. For each illustration the children did careful research. Chris chose my father's response to the question "What did it feel like to go back to the city you grew up in as a soldier?" (My father first returned to his hometown of Frankfurt, Germany, as a U.S. soldier and at the end of World War II discovered that his father had been deported to a concentration camp.) The quote Chris selected was "The city I grew up in was gone; it was flat. Then I found a few people, relatives and people who had known my father . . . I felt like an outsider. It was like coming to a strange country. It wasn't my country." Since Frankfurt had been heavily bombed, Chris searched books on World War II to find a picture of a bombed city. His resulting illustration mixes his imaginative ideas with my father's experience. The drawing depicts a nighttime scene with gray buildings and rubble, with my father in camouflage, a machine gun in his hand off to one side. Aly chose a quote where my father described the Henry Street Settlement House, where he first lived upon arriving in New York. Aly was able to find old photographs of the area and used them to illustrate my father's words. My father spoke of having to sell an expensive camera; Sam found pictures of old cameras to capture my father's experience. Once all the illustrations were done the children and I organized them so that they formed a coherent narrative and placed them on the bulletin board outside our room.

Student Interviews

I sent a letter home explaining our oral history project and asking for parents' help. One concern I had was getting a sufficient number of tape recorders. Fortunately, the school provided a few, several children brought in boom boxes and personal tape recorders, and a few parents lent small Dictaphone-type machines. In a few cases children did their interviews over the telephone using an answering machine's monitoring function to tape the interview. Before starting, each child was given a release form for the interviewees to sign and a "tips for interviewers" sheet. All the interviews were done after school and on weekends.

Student Transcriptions

Stephanie and I were concerned that the children would find transcribing a difficult task. For the first year I asked Dalton's learning specialist and an assistant teacher to help with the transcribing. For the transcription process, the class was divided into groups, each with an adult. We also collected a large number of old school cassette recorders and tried to find as many different rooms and hallways as possible so that the children would not be distracted by each other's tapes while transcribing. Remarkably, most children found the process relatively easy. The main difficulties were technical: tapes breaking (we raced to a store with one mangled tape to get it fixed so the child wouldn't have to redo the interview), poor sound quality, hard-to-understand accents. Eventually all the children transcribed their tapes successfully. Because the process went so smoothly the first year I did not feel the need for so many adults the second year. In fact, during the second-year transcription sessions I was usually alone with my class, and the children worked with great independence.

Student Picture Books

As soon as the children finished transcribing their tapes, we moved into a writing workshop mode. The children understood that they were to select quotes, create drafts of their story, revise it, and do final editing before beginning the illustrations.

The students approached the creation of a historical narrative in different ways. Some had lengthy transcripts and went through them with highlighters, selecting favorite quotes. Others used storyboards, outlines, and computers to structure their thinking, selecting quotes and doing simple sketches for each. Still others divided their transcripts into a series of quotes. One child decided to create a dual narrative: her caregiver's story and her own response to the story on facing pages. Most children combined quotes from the interview with a narrative of their own, always attempting to be true to the subject's story.

Drafting was essentially a process of creating a compelling narrative. Some children needed help keeping their stories simple, realizing that short quotes were often more emotionally worthwhile than long-winded ones. In several cases I helped children recognize the poetic elements in their transcripts. Sometimes they were concerned that their interviews were too sparse, yet some of these resulted in the most moving picture books. They worked with teachers and peers to consult, revise, and develop their books as they wished.

Illustrations varied depending on the children's abilities and interests. Colored pencils, markers, watercolors, and collage were all used. Several books included photographs. Titles were considered very carefully. In some cases, children selected a quote from the actual transcript. Others created titles that they felt best summed up their narratives. Each child was asked to select one page from the book to recreate as a poster. These small posters were exhibited in the room for the rest of the year, a historical record of the children's work long after the books had gone home.

I did several minilessons on possible book formats. Our models were several trade books I had discovered and, the second year, books created by the previous year's class. *Grandfather's Journey* by Allen Say was a model that many children used: pictures appeared on both sides of the page with the text at the bottom of each picture. Some chose a method created by a student in the first year: placing the quotes on one side of the page and the interviewer's comments on the other. Still other children placed the question on one side of the page and the answer on the other.

Children were encouraged to use a range of media and artistic methods. We looked at Jon Scieszka's *Math Curse,* Marissa Moss's *Amelia's Notebook,* Dia Cha's *Dia's Story Cloth,* and other books to consider different approaches to the art. Several children used collage; one used watercolor, crayon, and collage; most others used marker or colored pencil.

Chris's Book

A close look at how one child went through the project gives insight into the whole experience.

Chris is a good-natured child who enjoys school. He can become as easily involved in academics as he does in playful, silly behavior in the classroom and during recess. His reading and writing skills are still emerging, but he is conscientious, interested in learning, and eager to do well. As soon as we began discussing possible subjects Chris was certain: his baby-sitter was an immigrant. He would interview her. During morning and end-of-day meetings I would regularly check in with the class. Were they doing the interviews? Any problems? Chris said nothing, so I thought all was going well. When the interviews were completed, all the children brought their tapes to school to transcribe. Even then, Chris seemed to be doing well. However, before long things started to break down. He came to me in great distress. His baby-sitter had told him little. He didn't know how he would be able to create a story from the transcription. I took a look at his transcription, and saw that he had a point. She had been very terse with her answers, giving him almost nothing to work with. I suggested that he attempt to interview her again, to try other questions that might invite her to tell more.

The following day Chris's mother came to see me. It seemed that the baby-sitter was in a quandary, as was Chris. She had wanted to help Chris with his project because she was devoted to him. At the same time she was self-conscious about her English and her story and didn't want to tell Chris any more than absolutely necessary. Taking a close look at the transcription it was clear that this person was not the right one for Chris to interview. Even the second interview had not provided him with sufficient information with which to create a story. His mother told me she knew someone else, an acquaintance who might be willing to be interviewed. I said that would be great if Chris was willing to do the interview and transcription quickly, over a long weekend. I knew Chris would not want to fall too far behind the rest of the class. With a smile of relief, Chris went off, delighted that his problem had been solved. Within days he had done the interview with his new subject and quickly completed the transcription. His relief and joy transformed him. Now he was back on track, with a substantial story that he was certain that he could craft into a wonderful picture book.

Chris read his transcript over carefully, highlighting the quotes he planned to use in his book. He then created a storyboard of the narrative with quotes and sketches. Lastly, he did his final story in a commercially bound blank book. At every stage he made changes and additions. For example, much of his transcription is highlighted, though not all was used in the finished book. Asked about this, Chris told me that he chose certain parts because "I thought they all connected" and left out others because "they were extra." He eliminated some of the highlighted sections when creating his storyboard and still more when preparing the final version. For example, in his transcript he had highlighted the following:

> Well, it was overwhelming but I had already heard about it and seen lots of movies. My friends had been there and even my older sister was living there so it was not a big surprise. Wait, but the first time I came here it was 1968 and my plane landed and the snow started to fall so I went straight to my hotel and I did nothing. I was so tired. So I went to bed and I had a class on Wall Street the next day and when I woke up New York was totally covered in snow. All the streets were closed. The city was paralyzed. So that was the first day of my New York life.

For the storyboard Chris wrote:

> I came here. It was 1968 and my plane landed and the snow started to fall. So I went straight to my hotel and I did nothing. I was so tired so I went to bed. And I had a class on Wall Street the next day. And when I woke up New York was totally covered in snow. All the streets were closed . . . New York was paralyzed.

He included a sketch of an airplane flying across a city skyline with snow falling. For the final book he created a double-page spread with the skyline and airplane on the left and the stores and text on the right, all covered in falling snow. Chris explained to me that he had tightened up the story by cutting away extras. He was also proud of his use of ellipses at the end to provide, he felt, drama to the story.

In addition to extracting quotes to make a compelling narrative Chris added a short introduction. However, the power in the book lies in his pictures. Chris noticed the way his subject moved back and forth between New York and Paris and decided to use as a running motif a map of the Atlantic, with New York on one side and Paris on the other and a plane going one way or the other. "I think I got that little idea from cartoons," said Chris.

At the end of the unit Chris reflected on the experience in writing and in a conversation with me:

Q: What did you learn about immigration from this project?
A: I learned that America is a country of immigrants.

"I took my exam here and passed it. So I came here for the first time. I came for two months and I stayed in New York and I stayed in a hotel."

"Well to compare, well, I came from Paris, 2,000 years of civilization and I arrived in New York where everything is new. So 100 years old. Maybe 2,00. Those are totally different cities and are not comparable."

Q: What would you do differently [with the interview] if you did it again?

A: In the interview I learned a lot. I would not start with Nora. I think we should have asked her before we did it. I did not think Nora was comfortable with it because she didn't want to say anything. [If I did it again] I would just go to Marie Claude.

Q: What was your process in making the book?

A: I did a storyboard. I found things I liked, then wrote them down, and finally put them in order.

Q: What medium did you use for the illustrations?

A: Markers. I chose them because I thought I could fill up [the page] more with markers. I filled up as much as I could. At first I was going to keep one page white with the quote and one page all color with the picture, then I ended up filling up both pages with color.

Q: What did you learn about reading and writing from this project?

A: That a book that is good to read has to stick together and not just jump from one thing to another. I learned that to write a good story you need to write everything in a good order and the quotes have to fit together. I tried not to make it totally obvious that there were answers to different questions. I tried to blend it.

Q: What did you learn about history and being a historian?

A: I learned that when you are being a historian you can't spice up the quotes to make it a good story. I had to be careful that I didn't switch the story. That would change history.

Reflecting Back

My fourth-grade students learned a great deal from our oral history project on immigration—and so did I.

Content

In Chapter 1 I described my overall teaching goals and my struggles in determining content. A good friend who read that chapter commented that I had no content goals. He and I had often discussed the issue of content: how to decide what was important to teach. I told him I was too uncertain about it to write about content. This book would, I hoped, be read by many different educators in different regions with different populations to teach. What might seem important to me as content for my upper-middle-class New York City children might seem unimportant to a teacher in a strikingly different environment. However, on completing the immigration unit and throughout the months that followed, it was evident that my students had indeed learned a great deal of content information about immigration. Ellis Island was now much more than a symbol to my students, Charlie Chaplin an immigrant artist they knew well. My students now knew that immigrants came to America for many reasons other than those that had motivated their own families. They also understood the controversies surrounding immigration today. Many of them noted in their self-evaluations that they had learned more about the intricacies of citizenship as a result of the unit. Some even pointed out that now they knew the difference between the terms *emigration* and *immigration*.

Research Skills

My students also learned a great deal about what it meant to collect information and use it in an original work. They learned to create questions for an interview, to tape and transcribe an interview, to extract significant quotes from a transcription, to organize those quotes into a coherent historical narrative, and to illustrate that narrative.

Sensitivity

My students and I learned an enormous amount about being sensitive to people's need for privacy. I had been so concerned not to impose a family history project on my students that I had not considered that others outside their families might also feel uncomfortable having their lives investigated. In particular, Chris's story made me realize that in my zeal to validate the people who worked for and around my students I hadn't considered their right to privacy sufficiently. As I thought back over the first year of the project I realized that students who had come up with short interviews with little information were often dealing with subjects who were very ambivalent about being interviewed. The interviewees often wanted to help the children, but at the same time didn't want to expose too much of their own lives. At the time, I had attributed most of these brief interviews to my students' weak interviewing skills rather than to reluctant subjects. It was only with Chris's problem that I became aware of what an imposition this project can be. In the future I will attempt to be more conscious and more sensitive to how these interviews can intrude on a subject's privacy and help my students be more aware of this possibility as well.

Empathy

I think that all who were involved in the oral history project developed empathy in the course of the unit. My students certainly did so as they conducted the interviews and constructed the immigrant picture books. I believe the interview subjects, the parents, and the other teachers also enhanced their feelings for others as they listened to and read the stories.

Logistics

Competence with logistics may seem to some unimportant to learning, but I disagree. My students and I learned a lot about organization, about how best to conduct and record interviews. Many of my students' comments in their final self-evaluations addressed the issue of organization and logistics. Some said that if they had it to do over, they would "use a better tape recorder" or "plan the interview better."

Children as Oral Historians

The students and I learned that conducting interviews is a wonderful way to be a historian. Certainly, my experience has made me an advocate. I think oral history is one of the best ways to bring young children into the process of doing history. I am sure it can be done with any topic. I happened to use immigration, but I'm sure local history, World War II, the Vietnam War, or some other historical topic could work equally well.

■ ■ ■

Our formal presentations in the library over, we meander down to Room 909 for refreshments. I chat with grandparents who tell me that their grandchildren have been able to tell their stories unlike anyone else, with baby-sitters delighted by the sudden attention, with parents awed by their children's artwork and careful historical recording. The guests wander about the room, admiring the documents of our immigration studies: posters advertising the picture books, photomontages of our trip to lower Manhattan, charts full of comments about history and immigration. The children excitedly run for the refreshments they had set out earlier. The room is decorated in red, white, and blue. As I talk and watch, I also think to myself, This is why we create histories, to remember and honor ordinary people's lives.

 Zooming In

Designing an Oral History Project

The appeal of doing oral history with children is that it makes learning history an active experience: children are actually doing historical research. It also serves as a corrective to the broad picture normally presented in textbooks and standard historical accounts. It takes the learning of history out of the classroom and draws on the immediate experiences of children. While some might question the extent to which elementary school children can conduct legitimate oral history interviews, personal experience with fourth graders, reports from colleagues over the years, and published accounts of student projects have shown that it is a project worth undertaking. Doing an oral history project encourages students to work cooperatively to generate questions and contribute to the group learning experience, provides opportunities for independent learning, and presents children with new experiences. Furthermore, as Sitton, Mehaffy, and Davis suggest, "Oral history fieldwork has direct application to the students' day-to-day life in society, their perennial career as social newcomers" (1983, p. 19).

Selecting a topic for an oral history project can be done in a number of ways. The class can decide as a whole what topics to pursue. Recent historical events, local history, and family history are some of the topics you might consider to support your curriculum. In one middle school classroom, a teacher used an oral history project to allow students to pursue topics of individual interest. Students selected individuals that the students wanted to get to know better—members of their family, friends, neighbors, people in various professions, or local community leaders. Each of the students worked to find ways to make the experience of a particular individual interesting to an audience of their peers. They also worked with the completed collection of stories, by discussing both the significance of individual experiences as well as the conclusions that could be drawn from the stories as a single set of historical data. Discussing problems involved in representation and the selective nature of historical evidence was central to the students' analysis of the completed interviews. Students were also asked to think about the challenges of evaluating a data set constructed around their personal interests and the availability of subjects. The issue of how the selection of different subjects might change the picture led to a discussion about the way a historian's work is influenced by the selection of data.

 Booktalk

Oh, Freedom! Kids Talk About the Civil Rights Movement with the People Who Made It Happen
by Casey King and Linda Barrett Osborne

In 1989, Casey King, a fourth- and fifth-grade teacher in an inner-city integrated school, was surprised to discover how little his students knew about the civil rights movement. This inspired him to have his students write their own history based on the personal experiences of people they knew. The resulting extraordinary volume (King and Osborne 1997) presents the results of this collaborative project between a classroom teacher, a parent, and the students. It captures the voices of family members, friends, and neighbors who participated in the civil rights movement, as recorded by fourth and fifth graders working as oral historians. Thirty-one interviews were selected from more than 2,000 pages of stories recorded over a seven-year period by a large group of students at St. Anthony's, an integrated Washington, D.C., school. Though the selections are brief, each one captures an element of the personal experiences of the interviewees. Three historical essays—on life during segregated times, on the movement to end segregation, and on the extension of the movement to end both discrimination and poverty—place the interviews in context, as do historic and contemporary photographs of the subjects and the students. A time line of significant events of the civil rights movement, from the 1954 ruling by the Supreme Court on *Brown v. Board of Education* to the death of Martin Luther King in 1968, rounds out the picture. Students particularly interested in civil rights can investigate further topics of interest using the bibliography as a guide. Also available is a four-page classroom guide, which outlines the methods used by Casey King in the construction of this oral history project.

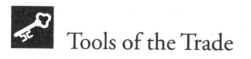 Tools of the Trade

Using Audio Evidence

With the growing importance and ready availability of video for classroom use, the use of audio material may be overlooked. Listening to speeches, recordings of oral history interviews, old radio shows on topics of interest, and reports from current public radio shows can help students develop their listening skills as well as their analytic abilities. It is also an excellent way to prepare them for the analysis of their own oral history tapes. Try having students listen to a fifteen- to twenty-minute segment of a tape and then write a brief summary of what they heard. Distribute a list of questions related to the subject before the class listens, and ask them to predict how having that list will change the experience of listening. You can also have them use commercial tapes to practice transcription.

Audio cassettes are available through multimedia catalogs distributed to schools and catalogs from public radio stations and museums such as the Smithsonian. Some resources may also be available on CD, which may in the future become a more readily available format. Another source for audio material is through the Internet. Currently, the American Memory collection of the Library of Congress has a few selections that can be downloaded, with many other selections to become available in the next few years. Other such sites are expected in the near future.

Researching On-Line

With the growing popularity of oral history as a teaching tool, there has been a proliferation of resources on oral history, many of which are available on-line. You can access essays that provide background information, sites that feature oral history interviews, as well as bibliographies and "how-to" instructions. Using two or three of the best sites in combination can yield all the material you would need to construct a complete oral history project.

Go to the Utah State University Oral History program educational resources (address below) and read or download essays on the significance of oral history and a brief essay on how to collect oral histories. Download "Tips for Interviewers," a widely reproduced set of guidelines for conducting an interview written by noted oral historian Willa K. Baum. You can distribute this to older students as is, or simplify the instructions for younger students. Use the one-minute guide to conducting an oral history interview from the University of California, Berkeley, Regional Oral History Office and Library Web page. Go to the History and Social Studies Web page mentioned in Chapter 1 to find a list of many additional sources for oral history materials.

For resources on immigration, particularly historic places that provide visual images of twentieth-century immigration to New York, look at sites for Ellis Island and the Tenement Museum. You can connect to several locations to learn how the island was used as a major processing center for immigrants from the turn of the century to its closing 1954. Audio clips of the remembrances of immigrants can be found on both the 1-Channel and the History Channel Ellis Island Web sites, as well as many evocative photographs of the buildings and people who passed through Ellis Island. There are also links to other related Web sites, including a collection of historic photographs of Ellis Island from the California Museum of Photography.

The site featuring the Tenement Museum does a superb job of conveying the immigrant experience of the poor on the Lower East Side of New York. More than 10,000 people lived in the tenement building at 97 Orchard Street from the time it was built until the time it was sealed because of violations to new housing laws in 1935. When restoration began in 1987 more than 1,500 objects were found in the building. Two restored apartments were opened to the public in 1994. Many of the objects found in the renovation are on display, as are furnishings and wall coverings.

The Web site allows a distant visitor to make a virtual tour of the apartments of two families, a German Jewish family that lived in the building in the 1870s and an Italian Catholic family that lived there in 1915. You can also see rooms of a model that has been constructed to depict life on each floor of the building. You can excavate layers of wallpaper and can even uncover ten objects found hidden beneath the floorboards. The site also has a detailed historical essay.

Here are the addresses for the sites described in this section:

Utah State University Program in Oral History:
 http://www.usu.edu/~oralhist/edu.html
University of California, Berkeley, Regional Oral History Office and Library Web page:
 http://www.lib.berkeley.edu/BANC/ROHO/rohotips.html *and*
 http://www.lib.berkeley.edu/BANC/ROHO/1minute.html
History and Social Studies Web page:
 www.execpc.com/~dboals/a-part2a.html/
I-Channel Ellis Island page: http://www.i-channel.com/ellis/
Ellis Island: http://www.ellisisland.org
History Channel Ellis Island page:
 http://www.historychannel.com/historychannel/ellisisle/newworld.html
Tenement Museum http://www.wnet.org/tenement/

far Away: Studying Native Americans from the Outside

It is our first day back in January. Cold and gray it may be outside, but Room 909 is bursting with life. The bulletin boards and walls are covered: Cinderella stories, illustrations from our immigrant oral history project, maps of Big Dalton, immigration ABC posters. Charts documenting conversations about history, about literature, and about other aspects of our studies abound. The reading corner is still full of the pillows I put there in September—but those pillows are now carefully piled up in a configuration designed by the children, not me. Nearby, now part of our classroom library, are the immigrant oral history picture books. Cubbies are full of kid stuff: folders, books, special pencils, click erasers (boy, do I hate them!), stuffed animals, key chains, and the like. On the door is a child's wonderful welcoming cartoon of the class. The room is no longer mine, but ours.

At the morning meeting we go over our usual routine: attendance, announcements, the daily schedule, a student read-aloud. Then I ask the children to get new folders. I begin to introduce our new history unit. "I love this time of year. It may be gloomy outside, but we can get so much done inside. We have January, February, and March—a long block of time for a big project. It will be on the first immigrants to this continent: American Indians."

"Native Americans, Ms. Edinger."

"Oops, I'm sorry, Native Americans. However, you know, Native Americans have told me that when not using their tribal name they use American Indian. And Canadians say First People. So I tend to mix the terms. Anyway, as I was saying, we will be delving deeply into a Native American culture—"

"But we learned this already."

"What do you mean? You've already studied the Kwakiutl?"

"No. But last year our class did the Iroquois. We read Sign of the Beaver *and made a mural."*

"That's great, but they aren't the same as the Northwest Coast people, you'll see."

"My class did the Aztecs last year and *the Woodland Indians in second grade. Are they the same? My mother said she would scream if we made another model of an Indian village."*

"Don't worry, they are all totally different."

"Our class studied Marco Polo and India last year."

"Well, there you are. Indians aren't Native Americans."

"But we did Native Americans when I was littler; I remember one year making Hopi sandpaintings for Thanksgiving."

"Aren't sandpaintings Navajo?"

"Ours were Hopi and fun to make. We've all done enough on Native Americans. This is going to be boring."

I take a deep breath. This is a conversation I'm used to. When I began teaching in-depth units on American Indians, my students came to me without much previous school experience on them. However, just as I changed so did the lower school teachers. For the last few years, my students had indeed been exposed to Native American cultures in various ways: through the changing second- and third-grade curricula, through multicultural holiday activities, through special events such as a PTA multicultural fair, and through individual teachers' well-intentioned, but misinformed, activities such as the sandpaintings. "Well, I hope this new unit won't be boring. I actually think it really is interesting. How about if we begin by you telling me what you already know about Native Americans? That way I can be sure that it isn't the same as what you've done before." I give out a survey with open-ended questions designed to give the children a way to indicate to me what they already know and what they may still want to know about Native Americans.

After school, as I read through the surveys, I know I have my work cut out for me. My students' written comments show enormous gaps, stereotypes, and misinformation despite their opinion that they already have "done" Native Americans.

"Native Americans hunt every day for food and they use animal skin for clothing especially beaver."

"[I want to] learn more about how they live, how they communicate, and their gods."

"Native Americans live on the East or West coast. Each tribe lives in a village. They have very hard lives hunting, sewing, finding clothes."

"I remember in a book I read this person I don't remember if it was an Indian had to run for cover while Indians threw things at him for a test."

"[Today] they live in Indian villages."

"[I want to know] how old you had to be to do the thing where you stay by yourself for a couple of days without any supplies."

"I know that some Indians live in wigwams, some live in teepees, and some live in longhouses. Some live in Mexico."

"I know they have very different views than other people."

"[I want to know] how they lived."

"[Last year] I learned that the Indians were kicked out and invented a lot of sports."

"Some live like us, but others live in camps and live like real Native Americans."

"[I know that] they used to sacrifice people to God."

"[I want to know] more about their hobbies."

My students are middle-class and New Yorkers to the core. Most are European American, a few are Asian and African American. None are Native American, nor have they had any direct contact with Native Americans. They know what they know of Native Americans through school and the media. And what they know seems stereotypic, mythic, and muddled. I sit back and think about how hard it is to learn about the history of cultures different and distant from our own.

Howard Gardner, in *The Unschooled Mind* (1991), describes how scripts, stereotypes and misconceptions learned by young children are hard to dislodge by subsequent schooling. He writes, "Whereas students are sometimes unable to relate a text to their own experiences, at other times students prove unable to distance texts from their own often-idiosyncratic assumptions about human nature. A major biasing factor stems from the simple schemes about human behavior that were developed in early childhood on the basis of interactions with others in the environment. For example, as children they learned to trust certain people and teachers, and in later years they assume that anything told them by a trusted parent or teacher is accurate and exhaustive" (p. 174). My survey results and the students' comments made it clear to me that my students' knowledge of Native Americans was quite stereotypic and would be difficult to confront. I too grew up with stereotypic knowledge about Native Americans. Born in the 1950s, I well remember watching Roy Rogers and playing Cowboys and Indians with my friends. There were no Native Americans where we lived. I acquired certain information so innocently that for years I didn't know it was incorrect. For example, my family traveled and camped a great deal when I was young. Often we used outhouses, which my parents called "Indian toilets" perhaps because outhouses were prevalent in the American Indian areas we visited. It was only as an adult that I realized that this was my parents' term, not an accepted alternative term for outhouses.

Gardner writes of the power of trusted adults, but the media are another important source of information. On television my students may have watched old cartoons with Porky Pig dressed as an Indian chanting, "Kill the wabbit! Kill the wabbit!" There is Disney's *Pocahontas* with a romanticized view of a true story. The media, well-intentioned but limited school experiences, and an environment far away from real-life native people all conspire to sustain my students' highly stereotypic ideas about Native Americans today and historically.

As I began focusing on how to better teach about Native Americans in U.S. history I looked at how other teachers did it. It seemed that there were three major approaches: multiple small engagements, a large unit that generalized about all Native Americans, and an in-depth look at one Native American group. I rejected the multiple small engagements approach immediately because it was antithetical to my personal teaching style. I just had never liked short lessons on anything; I liked long-term projects. My first effort was to begin our study of U.S. history with a unit focusing on Native Americans by region. I divided my class into five groups: Northeast, Northwest, Southeast, Southwest, and Plains. Each group researched the people of their region and presented their results to the class. I recall a model of a longhouse done by the Northeastern group and a skit with masks by the Northwest Coast group. However, this approach struck me as rather superficial and didn't seem to help my students in their subsequent studies of U.S. history. Native Americans seemed to take the same place as victims and marginalized people as they had in previous years when I had used only the textbook. I decided that a better approach would be an in-depth look at one area. I began with the Southwest because I traveled there, had firsthand information, and was able to get a lot of age-appropriate material for my students during my visit to the area. After a couple of years I added the Maya and finally the Northwest Coast. In each case, I tried to have my students look deeply at each group of people. I hoped that these intensive studies would help my students confront and eliminate stereotypes and provide them with a foundation for more traditional U.S. history studies when they were older.

Due to Stephanie's influence, my focus for many years was more anthropological than historical. However, with the Northwest Coast unit I seriously considered the issue of history. The museum's exhibit "Chiefly Feasts" was about history: the history of the potlatch, how the Kwakiutl used their stories, art, and rituals to keep and tell their history. I saw the complexities that occurred when non–Native American scholars, explorers, and settlers came and misinterpreted events such as the potlatch. The result was tragic. The potlatch, an important ritual for Northwest Coast people, was outlawed for many years by outsiders. So history became a major theme in our Northwest Coast study. One of my passions became the idea of history. When I first taught the unit I focused on how art and myth were ways that Northwest Coast people represented their history.

I first taught the Northwest Coast unit during the 1992–93 school year. That year I built the unit around the museum's special exhibit. In subsequent years, I revised the unit each year with Stephanie's help. Each year's class had had different earlier experiences, so I adjusted my overall curriculum yearly. For the 1995–96 school year, I taught the unit immediately after the one on immigration. It consisted of five parts:

- History and myth
- Outsider learning: confronting stereotypic thinking
- Northwest Coast immersion
- Outsiders looking in: the research report
- Respectful appropriation: a New York City potlatch.

My Goals

In teaching a unit on Native Americans, I had several goals in mind:

- I hoped that by considering different ways of keeping history, by considering multiple perspectives and stories, my students would further deepen their personal definition of history. In particular, I hoped that they would see the way history is presented in myths and folktales—that it isn't always chronological, although it is the past. I wanted them to recognize that some cultures have radically different definitions of history, ones that may include supernatural events and beings.
- The children were challenged to become experts—historians—in a particular aspect of Northwest Coast life. Clearly, they weren't about to become university-level scholars, but they could become informed and knowledgeable at a level appropriate for their age and grade.
- This unit focused on various types of source material, and how facts about a group were collected and interpreted by others. The children had to sort through primary and secondary sources. A large part of the unit required them to be alert to the subjective quality of secondary source material. I also wanted them to come to respect and value nonwritten means of historical record keeping.
- In this unit I wanted the students to see that different didn't necessarily mean worse. It was hard for the children not to look at aspects of Northwestern Coastal life in the past and consider it somehow deficient. I wanted them to become conscious of their outsider status when researching a culture different from their own.

- My students easily see themselves as superior to other so-called "primitive cultures," rural people, people who aren't as well off as they are. They can easily feel pity; it is harder to get them to truly empathize. (It's also not easy for adults to do so.) When we look at Native American history it is hard not to feel pity. My goal was to move my students beyond pity to empathy.
- We make political decisions about people. For example, voting in a politician who would do away with welfare has profound implications for Native Americans. Knowing their history and empathizing with their contemporary situation is important. As we read of Native Americans setting up casinos, or of large numbers of them living in poverty, it is clear that knowing their past affects how we consider their present and future. This unit would, I hoped, help my students view the media's presentation of Native Americans more thoughtfully than previously.

History and Myth

During the 1996–97 school year my students and I talked regularly about history. When we began the Northwest Coast unit I asked the children to review their ideas about history and who tells it. In particular, I asked them to consider what it meant to have someone outside your culture tell your history. How would they feel, I asked them, if someone from far away told about their family history and got it wrong? What if this outsider looked at old photos and totally misinterpreted the scene? As my students got more and more involved in Northwest Coast culture, issues of being outside a culture constantly came up. We learned that many of the Northwest Coast groups, before white people came, had well-established ways of keeping their own histories, which involved dance, myth, and art. Stephanie did many lessons with us, using artifacts, slides, and museum visits to help us see different, nonwritten ways of keeping history.

Outsider Learning: Confronting Stereotypic Thinking

Calling attention to stereotypic thinking about Native Americans was an important element of my teaching during the unit. I struggled with how best to do so. I knew that my students respected me and that whatever I presented would hold great weight (until, perhaps, another respected teacher in their future would give them something that would replace it). But I was uncomfortable with my role of know-it-all. I wanted to balance my pointing out to them the stereotypic way many experts had written about Native Americans with the children's own discovery of it. I decided to begin with a lesson that showed how a text, created by a much-admired outsider to the culture, reinforced stereotypes. My intention was to model for my students a way of looking critically at texts that would help them become aware of the potential for such stereotyping in the texts they would subsequently encounter during the unit.

One day at the beginning of the unit I asked my students to sit around me for a read-aloud. As soon as I held up Susan Jeffers's book *Brother Eagle, Sister Sky,* Ben said, "I know that book. It is great!" Other children concurred.

"Yes. This is a very beautiful book," I agreed. "Susan Jeffers did take a lot of time to research it and make it beautiful. But you know what? Despite its beauty and her careful work, it has some serious problems. The book is based on a version of a speech given by a real person, Chief Seattle, in 1853 or 1854 at a meeting with Governor Isaac Stevens, who wanted the chief to sell his tribal lands and move his people to a reservation. Listening to the speech was a man named Henry Smith, who took notes and then many years later wrote his version of the speech. Here are some pictures of Chief Seattle and his people." I showed the class *Chief Seattle,* a small book compiled by David Buerge containing excerpts from Smith's rendition and photographs of the Chief and his people. "Let me read you some of Smith's version of the speech."

I read the excerpts where Chief Seattle talks of how he witnessed the arrival of the first white people as a child and subsequently saw the destruction they caused to his people and their way of life. "How terrible," remarked Rachel. "He talks so much about the loss of his land to the white people. He sounds sad and angry."

"I don't blame him," said David. "I'd be upset too."

"So you can see that our best source on Chief Seattle's speech is Henry Smith's version," I said. "According to this version, Seattle talks about nature in terms of losing his land to the whites. Susan Jeffers used a different source, a version written in the 1970s that seems to have a different theme. Let me read you her version. See if you can figure out what the theme is and how it differs from Smith's version." I read the Jeffers book aloud, showing the children the gorgeous illustrations that fill the pages.

"Those look like Plains Indians in that picture. Did the Northwest Coast people use horses?"

"Actually, no, they didn't," I replied. "Jeffers decided to illustrate many Native American groups, not just those of the Northwest Coast."

"That's weird. It should be like the other book, with pictures of Chief Seattle and his people, not all those other groups."

"I don't get it. This book is totally different. It isn't about the whites taking away land. It's about us destroying the environment. And what is that last page supposed to mean, with that family and the ghost Indians behind them?"

I end with Jeffers's afterword: "To all of the Native American people, every creature and part of the earth was sacred; it was their belief that to waste or destroy nature and its wonders is to destroy life itself. Their words were not understood in their time. Now they haunt us. Now they have come true, and before it is too late we must listen."

"Wow. I still think it is a beautiful book, but I don't know if she had the right to change the Chief's words."

"I don't know either."

"It makes me very uncomfortable. I don't think we have the right to change someone's message to fit one of ours."

"Native Americans often talk about nature, so we often seem to use them as symbols of saving the environment. But is that right?"

"I don't know. I really love the book, but I can see that she made Chief Seattle into something he wasn't."

"Boy, you have to be really really careful when learning and writing about Native Americans if you aren't one. It is so easy to write about them in the wrong way."

Northwest Coast Immersion

We human beings like to sort ourselves into groups. One way we often do so is to categorize people according to their physical proximity. Thus, the various ethnic groups who immigrated to the United States in the early twentieth century and first settled in the Lower East Side of Manhattan are called Eastern Europeans. However, they came from many different countries—Poland, Russia, and other countries in Europe. Similarly, Native Americans have been lumped together into regional cohorts. The regional unit I first developed and taught was on the Southwest. The first year I had my students research the Navajo and Hopi because they lived in the same area and I knew there was a lot of child-friendly material available on these groups. That year I, along with the children, learned of their differences. Indeed, the Hopi and Navajo have little in common: they are not descended from the same group of people, they have totally different cultures, and there is a history of tension between the two groups. Subsequently, I eliminated the Navajo and focused our studies on the Hopi and Pueblo, who did have more in common.

By the time I began to plan the Northwest Coast unit I knew it would be important to note the differences and similarities between the different tribes of the Northwest Coast. My main reason for having my students study several tribes in the area was practical. Stephanie and I spent a great deal of time seeking out research materials for the unit, and we discovered that there simply was not enough written for children on any one group. Therefore, we collected the best materials available on several groups: the Tsimshian, the Kwakiutl, the Tlingit, and the Makah. Throughout the unit we referred to the different tribes so that the children could see the commonalities and differences between the tribes.

Environment

The culture of the Northwest Coast tribes developed from their rich environment. Early on, Stephanie conducted a lesson using a collection of photographs that showed the variety and richness of the area: lush, temperate rain forests, rugged coastlines, inlets and bays, tall red cedars, salmon and sea otters—all could be found along the Northwest Coast region that stretched from Washington through Vancouver, British Columbia, to Alaska. She divided the class into small groups and gave each a photograph to study. After a while she asked them to describe the photographs for the whole class, and she wrote the comments on a class chart. This experience allowed for multiple interpretations of the same subject and enabled each child to construct his or her own picture of the physical place inhabited by the people they were studying. Later, as the children did their individual research, they would come across similar images in the materials they were using. Excited, they would wait for Stephanie to arrive so they could point out to her the similarities between what she had presented and what they had found; sometimes they even came across the same images as Stephanie had shown.

Artifacts

Stephanie has access to a remarkable collection of artifacts, and one day she brought some of her Northwest Coast materials to my class. We sat in a circle, and she passed around each artifact for us to touch and study closely. She then asked us what we thought the object was and how it was used. Identifying some artifacts was easy, such as the tribes' small, beautifully constructed clothespin dolls, which helped familiarize us with the traditional clothing of the Northwest Coast, such as button blankets, and musical instruments, such as drums, rattles, and whistles. The purpose of other objects was less obvious, such as the beautifully decorated grease dish (we did not yet know that grease was a food delicacy for the Northwest Coast people). The cedar bark basket that Stephanie brought in helped us to appreciate the importance of cedar in Northwest Coast culture, and we marveled at the way the bentwood box was constructed.

Later in the unit we visited the Northwest Coast Hall at the American Museum of Natural History. Stephanie prepared a worksheet that enabled the children to explore their own interests while we were there. For example, she asked them to find a mask to draw, and they excitedly moved about the hall seeking out their favorites. Seeing the enormous totem poles after studying them was also a great pleasure.

In a museum classroom Stephanie produced more artifacts, most notably a huge transformation mask, which was several feet long. The children were delighted when Stephanie put it on and showed them how it worked. However, our favorite museum artifact had to be the dollhouse-sized model of a Kwakiutl house. Stephanie had the children put it together, beginning with the interior materials and moving on to the house poles and lastly the roof.

The opportunity to handle and view actual Northwest Coast artifacts helped to make these distant people far more real to my students.

Outsiders Looking In: The Research Report

I have always enjoyed research projects. Throughout my teaching career, wherever and whatever I taught, I always found a way to create a research unit. Collecting the data and structuring the unit was always fun. More difficult, however, was helping children with the writing. My students would collect lots of information on a topic, sometimes of their own choosing, and would then attempt to mold it into a piece of nonfiction, often expository, writing. Tremendous emphasis was given to the avoidance of plagiarism by being original (a bit ironic, since such writing can be markedly uncreative). I remember my own fourth-grade butterfly research: sitting with several books open in front of me, one an encyclopedia volume, contentedly paraphrasing sentence after sentence for the report. Length was no problem. Not long enough? I went to the library and found another book with a little more data. I have pleasant memories of taking almost as long to create an attractive cover (note: drinking straws make great butterflies) as to write the report. I was very happy with the final product: it looked great, it was long, and it got me a good grade.

More recently, many educators have reworked the research report paradigm by inviting children to select their own topics and by valuing process over product. However, ownership of a topic and emphasis on process does not automatically mean the end of old ways: I've observed students with self-selected topics simplistically paraphrase out of books, spend an excessive amount of time on covers, and be overly concerned with length. I have found that, in addition to children owning their topics and working within a process-centered classroom, they need to keep in mind why and for whom they are writing. *Audience* is the missing piece; it makes the ownership worthwhile, the process compelling. Who is going to read my report? How do I write it for that person or group of people? Additionally, the children need to feel that there is a driving reason to do the report. It needs to be more than an exercise in learning; they need to feel that what they are doing has a real purpose.

For the Northwest Coast research paper, I invited the children from the start to think of themselves as serious researchers. They would be functioning as scholars, doing work that was important and meaningful. They were asked to continually keep in mind who would be reading their work (their peers, teachers, and family would be the primary audience). Finally, they were asked to create a piece of writing as accurate as possible, one that could be approved by a member of one of the Northwest Coast tribes.

Topic Selection

In order to encourage the children to consider selecting research topics outside their previous experience, I prepared research folders on a large variety of topics. Each folder contained reading material from texts that were up to date, interesting, and at a reading level all the children could manage. I came up with the topics based on the research materials available. Stephanie and I worked hard to find readable, accurate materials for the children. For example, one of my sources was a teacher's guide for a reading series created for children on Queen Charlotte Island. Stephanie explored the Internet and found wonderful bibliographic information at the U'Mista Cultural Society site. (An annotated bibliography of the materials we found is in the appendix.) Topics I selected included Art, Canoes, Clans, Eulachon, Household Articles, Kwakiutl Legends, Rituals, Winter Ceremonies, Bentwood Boxes, Cedar, Contact with Whites,

Fishing, Houses, Masks, Shamans, Tools, Button Blankets, Ceremonial Regalia, Environment, Food, Potlatches, Spirits, and Totem Poles. After the children had acquired some background on the people of the Northwest Coast I invited them to select their research topics. They rummaged through the topic folders, looked at the books on display in the room, and considered their own personal interests.

Doing Research

Once topic selection was completed our focus turned to research. In directed lessons, I modeled different aspects of the research process, from initial note taking to drafting. I worked closely with the children to help them figure out which research method worked best for them. During this time, the children joined in, describing their own methods and techniques to the class during minilessons just as I had. For example, one child explained his technique of color coding his notes. Another described her need to write multiple drafts to figure out what she really knew and wanted to say. Still another child did elaborate outlines before writing her first draft. All worked as peer advisors in response groups and individual conferences.

Writing

Writing the report proved to be one of the hardest parts of the project for the children. Despite all my efforts, their tendency was to copy from reference materials and paraphrase their notes for their final report. I worked hard to help them create a personal voice. The usual writing-process procedures stayed in place: minilessons, conferring, sharing. Each child needed his or her own kind of help. Some needed a teacher checking in every day, while others worked with great independence, only wanting comments late in the process. Still others would demand constant reassurance from adults that their work was acceptable. These children were encouraged to work with greater independence. In some cases, they were not allowed to show any work to us until they had done two complete drafts. Children worked as peer editors, too, responding to friends' work in groups and individually.

The children ultimately became experts on their chosen topics through their research and writing. The final reports were the tangible evidence of their expertise. They ranged greatly in style, since the children had tried hard to make them interesting for their audience of peers, parents, and teachers as well as acceptable to a member of a Northwest Coast tribe. In some cases, the children inadvertently used stereotypes in their efforts to be creative. One year, a child wrote her report in the voice of an imaginary chief with a stereotypic name. I encouraged her to do further research on names. However, she balked, feeling it interfered with her creativity. Because we felt the children owned their writing, we could only suggest, never insist. In such cases, some children were delighted to have us point out stereotypes and willingly revised their pieces; others refused. Each situation had to be considered individually. For example, one child did a superb job researching shamans, but then undercut her work by writing her piece in the voice of a shaman. She was very proud of her report, and we did not want to undermine her self-esteem by pointing out the problems with this approach. I accepted that the children, while more aware of stereotypes by the end of the unit, were still outsiders to the culture and would not get rid of all their stereotypes after only a few weeks of study.

Karen's Report

Karen was an enthusiastic and confident learner and leader. Her social self-confidence never ceased to amaze me. She oversaw her friends and our classroom, and tried to oversee me too at every opportunity. Karen was as tenacious about academics as she was about everything else. A perfectionist, anxious about deadlines, Karen invariably was the first person finished with any project. Learning to sit back or take time with her work was not Karen's learning style at all. She liked to write, but she had no previous experience with the writing-process approach. Her idea of writing was for me to give her the assignment, Karen to write a draft, me to correct the grammar, and Karen to write a final, neat copy. Wham, done, and on to the next was Karen's methodology.

With the Northwest Coast research report our skirmishes escalated into a major war, as I determined to bring Karen to a new level as a writer and she became just as determined to continue as she had. I knew Karen had potential as a writer. Her ideas were good and she had decent basic skills, but she needed to learn how to seriously draft and revise. Karen had been selling herself short as a writer. Her rushed method did not provide her with the means to find her voice or her style, something I was certain she was capable of. Additionally, I knew she would gain a deeper understanding of her topic if she lived with it a bit longer than she was accustomed to doing.

At the start of the unit, when asked about her previous experience with Native Americans, Karen wrote, "Last year we studied Aztecs and their surroundings. We had two big projects. 1. We were assigned a topic and tried to find as much research as possible and turn them into your own words. 2. A group project." Further conversation with Karen revealed that the research project had been very set. The teacher told the children what to do at every step of the way. Karen felt it had been a large project she had done very well. As a result, she began her Northwest Coast research project certain that she knew all there was to know about researching and writing about a Native American topic.

Karen selected Houses as her topic—an interesting one because of the beauty of the old longhouses and how they were made. I had a great deal of excellent material for Karen to use, and she sat down with a tremendous sense of independence to begin her research. When I first checked in with her she had several pages of written material. As I read through her work I noted a mixture of clearly copied information and sentences that seemed like her own. At the top of her first page, Karen had written:

The Northwest Coast Indians were very smart people one thing they taught themselves to do was building a house. The house is made out of cedar logs. There are four basic pieces that you need to build a house from, but many of each of them.

Drawings followed, and more information. Karen then informed me that she was taking notes and writing the report all at once. I explained to her that she couldn't do this, that she needed to collect the data first and then use that information to write a piece of her own. Storm clouds came across her face as she announced, "You have your way of working, and this is my way of working."

"But Karen, this isn't about different research styles, but basic to all kinds of research. You can't write your own piece at the same time as taking notes."

"This is how we learned to do it last year."

Changing tack, I took a look at her work. I pointed out that a lot of information seemed to be missing and showed her where she might get more. This Karen grudgingly accepted and moved on to take more notes.

Her next step was to begin writing her report on one of the portable word processors we had. Her first draft read as follows:

The Northwest Coast Indians were very smart people. They had their own way of living and building. The Northwest Coast Indians housing plan was unbelievable. They were strong and steady and prepared for weather. The materials were simple cedar. The wood was not cut by a saw or anything like that the cedar was pried off. It consisted of one large room in the center there was a fire place and the smoke was able to leave the house because the house was made of wood planks that were able to

---

move. There were four basic shapes to build a house. Many strong men are needed to build a house and strengths of different ropes. In the house there was only one floor, but most of the time the house was way down into the ground and steps were formed totem poles were used to hold up for roof support.

Karen was very pleased with her first draft and was quite put out with me when I was not prepared to do a final edit so she could move on to her final draft. Grumpily, she listened to me suggest that she organize some paragraphs and add some additional information on building materials, types of houses, and how the houses were organized. I also reminded her that the Northwest Coast people used to live in such houses, but today they lived in contemporary houses and she might want to make that clear in her piece.

After some effort, Karen produced her second draft:

The Northwest Coast Indians were very smart people. They had their own way of living and building. The Northwest Coast Indians housing plan was unbelievable. They were strong and steady and prepared for weather.

The materials were wood and medal adz, wood and bone adz, stone maul, wooden wedge, elbow adz.

The wood was not cut by a saw or anything like that the cedar was pried off. It consisted of one large room in the center there was a fire place and the smoke was able to leave the house because the house was made of wood planks that were able to move. There were four basic shapes to build a house. Many strong men are needed to build a house and strengths of different ropes. In the house there was only one floor, but most of the time the house was way down into the ground and steps were formed totem poles were used to hold up for roof support. The front of the house is decorated with the people's paintings that really finish the house. There are three different styles. The northern style, the central style, and the southern style. Each family had its own quarter of the house. In the summer the houses were moved to a warmer climate and were disassembled to be moved. Museums around the world own many of the totem poles that were made long ago. Tribes carved and painted poles in many sizes and used them for many purposes. The greatest totem poles were the ones that sat in the front of the house they were spectacular but things are not made like things were then.

At this point Karen decided to avoid me and try another adult in the room, the learning specialist who works in my writing workshop four days a week. To Karen's dismay, however, this adult did not consider the report complete and made some suggestions. Karen next took a collection of markers and used them to mark up her draft. Green highlighted her opening, which she clearly liked; yellow, orange, and pink were used to separate different sorts of information; brown indicated extraneous material to be deleted. Additionally, Karen penciled in additions.

She showed me this marked-up draft, certain she was now ready for publication even though she had made no substantive changes. At this point I took Karen out of the room for a serious heart-to-heart talk. I told her how certain I was that she could write an amazing report, but she might need to do several more drafts before it was done. We discussed the fact that everyone is a different kind of writer. I reminded her of E. B. White, an author we had studied, who did a great many drafts until he was satisfied with his writing. I also reminded her of my work, the many drafts I had shown the class of my writing.

The private talk seemed to be a turning point for Karen. She wanted to be a writer and now seemed to realize that it would take time. Now the idea of multiple drafts appealed to her, especially since she could do them on the computer. At this point, she would make printouts with every small addition and change, eager to show herself a serious writer, one who truly understood the idea of revision.

The result of Karen's efforts was the following final draft:

The Northwest Coast Indians were very smart people. They had their own way of living and building. The Northwest Coast Indians housing plan was something that only a genius could think of. They were strong and steady and prepared for weather. The houses were a very important thing to the Northwest Coast Indians.

The materials for building the houses were mostly hand tools. They included: wood and metal adz, wood and bone adz, stone maul, stone maul, wooden wedge, elbow adz.

Once the tree was chosen, wooden wedges would be hammered into the tree. the wood was cut down, then laid on a rack and chiseled off. The plank of the cedar was almost peeled off. Many strong men were needed to lift a single log.

The houses usually consisted of one large room. In the center there was a fireplace and the smoke was able to leave the house because the roof was made of wood planks that were able to move. There were no windows at all, just a little opening that was used as a door. In the house, there was only one floor, but most of the time the house was dug down into the ground and steps were formed. Totem poles were used to hold up the roof. The front of the house was decorated with the people's painting that really finished the house. There were three different styles of houses: the northern style, the central and southern style. Each family had its own quarter of the house.

This type of housing was about 100 years ago and today it is only used in ceremonies or in museums by Northwest Coast tribes. All of this information was taken from books that are on the Northwest Coast Indians.

In her self-evaluation, when asked what she had learned, Karen wrote, "Not only did I learn about the NW Coast Indians and how they lived and their houses and 'a lot of that,' but I think I learned about writing and how to be a writer and that length never matters. Draft after draft I struggled and until the last couple of drafts I didn't really think I could do it or make a real piece of writing."

A serious scholar, or even a more traditional teacher, might quibble about Karen's work. Her report lacks a great deal of information about longhouses. Perhaps a more traditional approach, using note cards and an outline, would have produced a more accurate report. However, I believe that Karen's struggles to understand what it is to do research, to take information and use it to craft a piece of her own helped her see herself as a writer. At the end of the year, Karen carefully placed every draft of her Northwest Coast research report in her presentation portfolio for fourth grade. She knew that she needed them all to tell the whole story of her writing "Northwest Coast Housing."

Respectful Appropriation:
A New York City Potlatch

"Chiefly Feasts," the museum exhibit that inspired my Northwest Coast unit, was about the potlatch, an important celebratory ceremony of the Northwest Coast native people. Potlatches can be held in honor of the raising of a totem pole, a wedding, or other special occasions. Guests are always given gifts by the host, and the event includes elaborate art, dances, and feasts.

When I began planning the unit with Stephanie, she brought me a third-grade curriculum for Native Alaskan children, which included lesson plans for a traditional Tlingit potlatch with an actual script along with instructions on how to make or procure the necessary regalia. I was troubled at the idea of our New York City children attempting to imitate something so unlike their own experiences and was concerned that trying to replicate the Northwest Coast tribal ceremony would do little to break down the children's stereotypic notions of Native Americans. After much conversation with Stephanie, we came up with the idea of a New York potlatch. This would be a ceremony based primarily on the Kwakiutl potlatch, but with the look and feel of New York City, our hometown. My hope was that the children would gain a deep knowledge and respect of the potlatch even as they adapted it to fit their own, urban life. With Stephanie guiding us, I collaborated with Al Preciado, an art teacher, and Joanna Brotman, a dance teacher, to make the potlatch a reality.

Social Structure

I began by reminding my class that they were a community like the Kwakiutl. Northwest Coast native communities place great emphasis on belonging to clans. Some groups, such as the Tlingit, are divided into two halves called moieties and then into clans; others, such as the Kwakiutl and Tsimshian, are just divided into clans. The Northwest Coast people have a strong connection to their environment and the animals that populate that environment. Their history is full of stories, myths, and traditions that place great value on the relationship between people and animals. Raven, Bear, Salmon, Wolf, Shark, and Otter are important Northwest Coast clans.

In considering themselves a community like the Kwakiutl or Tlingit, my students were helped to understand that, as a class, they could be divided into two moieties: themselves and their parents. The children's moiety would invite the parent's moiety to a potlatch. Within each moiety there would be four clans. In keeping with the New York City theme, great thought, energy, and discussion was spent on selecting urban animals for the moieties and clans. The children argued fiercely as to whether deer existed within New York City itself or only the suburbs, and whether pets counted, especially exotic or illegal ones like ferrets. Some years rodents and other pests were chosen in admiration of their tenacious survival in the city. Dog, Cat, Seagull, Frog, Turtle, Pigeon, Cockroach, Rat, Raccoon, Bee, Rabbit, and Owl were all significant clans and moieties over the years.

Totem Poles

We decided that our potlatch would be done in honor of the raising of clan totem poles. Totem poles were art, but also documents of a group's history. It was fascinating to learn how to read the poles and to learn the story that each told. Many different kinds of poles were created for different reasons. For our own class poles we worked with Al Preciado. For the first potlatch, Al worked as an art consultant in the classroom. He and I decided that the totem poles should be house poles, designed to stand in the four corners of the classroom. Since carving was out of the question in such a small space, cardboard, oak tag, construction paper, and paint were the materials used, and the children worked in the small classroom and hallway carefully cutting cardboard with matte knives and using hot glue guns and paint to create their poles. I thought the middle school director would never forgive us when we spilled paint all over the hallway carpet. There was also the matter of storage, which I thought I solved by tacking the totem pole sections on a bulletin board over the children's desks when they weren't working on them. How could I know that sections would fall, one narrowly missing a cupcake with a lit candle on it! Then there was the difficulty of living the rest of the year in constant fear of falling poles. Fortunately, after that first year, Al became a bona fide art teacher at the school and was able to work with the children in an art room that had a sink and storage. At subsequent potlatches the totem poles were raised in front of the headmaster's office, in the library, in the dance studio, and outside the art room, where they could be admired without the fear of falling.

Creation Myths

Understanding how stories, art, and myths can be forms of historical record keeping was an important aspect of the potlatch unit. I introduced the children to Northwest Coast mythology with a look at multiple versions of the myth "How Raven Got the Light." Then I challenged them to write creation myths for their clans. One year a group of children researched the school's founding and wrote a wonderful story that capitalized on their research yet kept the mythic element intact. For the first potlatch, the children performed their myths as plays. The following year the school added a dance program to the fourth grade, and Joanna Brotman, the dance teacher, agreed enthusiastically to participate and worked closely in subsequent years with the clans to help them choreograph their clan myths into dances. The children soon learned to appreciate the Northwest Coast peoples' view of their myths as a form of history. During Joanna's classes, the children focused on the special movements of their clan animals to create unique dances for their clans. Joanna was careful to avoid any stereotypic "Indian" movements and instead encouraged modern dance techniques, full of jumps and leaps.

I was always amazed at how well my students understood the idea of myth as history. The following two written myths are examples of what these fourth graders produced.

How the Raccoon Got Its Mask
by the Raccoon Clan

One day when Raccoon woke up he saw a small brook and decided to take a drink. Just before he took a drink he saw a black substance in the water but thought it was nothing. He sniffed the water. It smelled like oil. He put his head in. When he picked up his head he saw a new world before him. He tried to rub the substance off, but it wouldn't move. Soon he forgot about it and started to play. He built pyramids, and swam, but when he got out of the water, he heard a gun shot. Then he rolled over and died.

How the Hawks Became Friends to the People
by the Hawk Clan

Long ago there were very few people which enabled the hawks to fly freely where and when they pleased. But because of the lack of people the Transformer told all the hawks that she would bring more people unto the land by turning them into people. At first, the hawks were very annoyed by this because the people lessened their food supply and hunted them. After a while, however, most of the hawks liked the idea. So the Transformer turned the ones who wanted to be people into people.

One day the village chief (who was once a hawk) went hunting with his son. On their hunt they accidentally killed two hawks, which they brought to the Transformer in hopes that she would bring them back to life. The Transformer thought this was kind of them and in returned agreed to do so. The Transformer brought them back to life. When the hawks heard of this they welcomed the people to their land and formed a bond.

How the raccoon got it's Mask

Gifts

Traditionally, guests at a potlatch receive gifts as payment for witnessing the prestige of the hosts. In the past, woolen blankets, food, and household items were common gifts. I love looking at the wonderful old photographs of potlatches during the early part of the century with enormous piles of blankets and bags of flour ready to be given as gifts. For the class potlatch gifts, Stephanie and I showed the children samples of Northwest Coast artifacts from the museum's collections and from illustrations and postcards we collected. The children were encouraged to make variations of these objects as gifts. For example, the children made bent oak tag boxes after the bentwood boxes of the Northwest Coast. They also made minibutton blankets out of felt, sequins, construction paper, and paper dots. My favorite gifts were the crocheted and knitted pot holders one class decided to make. I had noticed that crocheted blankets were common gifts at contemporary potlatches and asked the children if they would like to learn to crochet and make pot holders as gifts. They loved the idea and had a bake sale to raise the funds for the materials. At first several children tried to knit, but eventually most gave up and crocheted instead. It was wonderful looking around the room that year as boys and girls helped each other to master the art of crocheting.

Regalia

Regalia are the ceremonial clothing and masks associated with Northwest Coast ceremonial life. Over the years I was particularly inspired by button blankets, made by different groups in the Northwest Coast. They are traditionally red and black or red and blue and are decorated with hundreds of white buttons that are placed in patterns on the blanket. The blankets tell stories just as totem poles do. They are, in fact, another type of historical document. Many of the students made button blankets to wear at their potlatches. One child's was so beautiful that it won a ribbon at a state fair the following summer. Sometimes children made simple masks to resemble their clan animals; however, they were nothing like the traditional ones of the Northwest Coast people. Those masks are a part of the stories owned by different Northwest Coast clans. The students, without ever voicing their feelings, clearly realized that imitating such masks would be disrespectful.

Potlatch Committees

As part of the preparation and planning for the potlatch, the children volunteered for different committees. There was an Invitation Committee, which was responsible for making and delivering invitations to all our special guests. A Gift Committee made gifts for these special guests (all the children made gifts for their parents). The members of the Speech Committee researched and prepared speeches for the potlatch. The children wrote a welcoming speech, a dance speech, a totem-pole-raising speech, a gift speech, and a feast speech. Lastly, there was a Feast Committee. This very popular committee planned the food for the potlatch and arranged for every member of the class to bring something. I insisted that the food be connected to the Northwest Coast and New York City. Thus, instead of barbecued salmon, we had bagels and lox spread, and instead of salmonberries or huckleberries, we had strawberries!

The Potlatch

The potlatch itself has been unique and wonderful every year. There was never the anxiety beforehand that a play sometimes creates. The children worked seriously and happily right up to the day of the event. They understood that it was a ceremony, that it could only happen once, and that it could only be a success. The first year the whole event took place in my small classroom. In following years the myth dances and speeches were presented in the dance studio, the totem-pole raisings in various locations in the school, and the gift giving and feast in the classroom. Every year the potlatch had its own unique character based on the personal interests and contributions of the participants. The potlatch not only served as a way to learn more about different ways of keeping history, about the Northwest Coast people, about ceremony, about art, and about dance, it also provided a community-building opportunity. As the students struggled in their clans to reach consensus on their totem poles and myth dance, they learned a great deal about how communities deal with conflict and disagreement.

Reflecting Back

I continue to struggle with how to help children learn about a culture that is distant and different from their own. I've rejected a holiday/food/clothing approach for something that I hope has more depth. However, I'm not totally convinced that my students gained a greater sense of distant and different people. For some, I believe the Northwest Coast unit did help them widen their idea of history to encompass non-Western notions of how people maintain and interpret their past. For others, I suspect that the unit may only have reinforced existing stereotypes of Native Americans.

For me, a white German-Jewish American teaching mostly white children of European extraction, it will always be a dilemma to teach about those different and far from ourselves.

■ ■ ■

March 1996. Totem poles raised, speeches given, dances performed, gifts distributed, feasting done, and research reports on display outside Room 909.

The Northwest Coast unit is over. "That was a great potlatch," one student marvels. The others murmur their agreement. We mull over what has been learned, trying to figure out what was most important. For some it was becoming an expert on a topic: canoes, button blankets, medicine. For others it was the skills of research: note taking, drafting, and revision. And for some it was learning about a culture from the outside:

- "The more you learn about the culture, the more you feel you're part of the culture, but you still know you'll never become part of it."
- "I learned that when you write something as an outsider you have to be careful and keep on rereading to make sure that you did not write incorrect or insulting information."
- "I don't think I am less of an outsider because I am not an Indian, am not related to one, but I do feel I know more about them."
- "Sometimes it felt almost weird. Yes, I think I became less of an outsider because now I know more about the culture."

Zooming In

What Is a Potlatch?

The potlatch is a ceremony held to celebrate significant ceremonial and social events among the native groups of the Northwest Coast. At the potlatch, the host distributes gifts lavishly to guests in order to enhance the prestige and status of the host and giver. Each potlatch consists of a display of the group's art and performances of specific dances and songs owned by the host family. The guests serve as witnesses, enjoying enormous feasts and receiving gifts that validate the status of the giver.

Historically, among the groups of the Northwest Coast, there were many different reasons for having a potlatch. Potlatches often were held at critical points in the life of an individual or a group—for example, at the naming of children, adoption, initiations, weddings, memorials, and the succession to an inherited leadership position. The various groups of the Northwest Coast had different rules for determining who the invited guests would be. The type of event celebrated would also play a role in determining the guest list.

What was most important at all potlatches, however, was that the guests witnessed the ceremony and accepted the gifts. The gifts distributed at a potlatch served as a kind of payment for the role the guests played at a potlatch as witnesses. The gifts were distributed to the guests in order of their rank. The more the host gave away, the more the host enhanced his prestige.

The kind of gifts distributed at potlatches has evolved, just as the potlatch has evolved, over time. Before the tribes' contact with white people, gifts consisted of prestige items, such as blankets of woven bark or animal skins, bentwood boxes, bowls, ladles, canoes, and food. By the late nineteenth century, Hudson Bay Company woolen blankets became common gifts. Occasionally coppers—or a small piece of a copper—an item of great prestige, were given away. During the early twentieth century, dishes, furniture, sewing machines, and fishing boats were among the prized items given away. Items given away at a modern potlatch include crocheted items, blankets, dishes and glassware, plastic containers, towels, and clothing. Potlatch was, and continues to be, an expensive undertaking that takes a long time to prepare and requires the support of an extended family group. During the nineteenth century, accumulating the property to be given away sometimes took many years. For the contemporary potlatch many gifts are purchased, but the quantity of items distributed still requires saving the money to make the purchases. Hosts must also insure that family members have the time necessary to make the handmade items that are still distributed. Today as in the past, even a very powerful chief can host only a few potlatches during his lifetime.

Rival chiefs who attend potlatches become obligated to host a potlatch in return. During the late nineteenth century, potlatch became very competitive, with some wealth being destroyed as a sign of tremendous affluence. Potlatch, however, benefited the whole community, not just the chief, since wealth was distributed to all the members of the society who attended.

Although potlatches were outlawed by the Canadian government in 1884, most groups continued to have potlatches in secret. The Kwakiutl in particular resisted longer than other groups the external forces that undermined the ceremony. Although the law outlawing potlatch was selectively enforced before 1922, only a few cases resulted in convictions. In 1922, however, an enormous potlatch was held and more than thirty people were arrested. Under the terms of the agreement reached by the court, many people surrendered their potlatch property, their regalia, and other precious items in exchange for suspended sentences. Others who refused to turn over their property were sent to prison. The arrests and confiscations meant that the potlatches, when held, were surrounded by even greater secrecy. Potlatches were often held around Christian holidays, such as Christmas, or conducted at remote locations. Another strategy was to hold a potlatch and divide the events over time, so that the ceremony was separated from the gift giving, making it harder to prove any connection between the events. Other factors that contributed to the decline of the potlatch included the Depression, an increase in missionary activity, changes in the fishing industry, and a lack of interest on the part of many younger members of the native groups. With an increased interest in the revival of native arts in the 1960s, potlatches also experienced a resurgence.

While traditional potlatches often lasted for several days, a modern potlatch might take place on one day, scheduled around a holiday. In the past, between performances of songs and dances, enormous feasts would be served to the guests. Feasts are still held at contemporary potlatches, but on a smaller scale. While traditional foods might include seal meat, salmon, venison, and berries, today a potlatch guest might be served salmon salad sandwiches and fish chowder.

If you were to be invited to a potlatch today, you would listen to speeches that describe a family's history, watch dramatic masked dances, and eat elaborate meals. While particular cultural practices have changed, the potlatch remains an important ceremony in the life of the Kwakiutl.

The story of the potlatch is an excellent way for students to understand the importance and tenaciousness of cultural practices. Although the potlatch has changed over time, its endurance and resurgence provides an excellent example of a culture evolving over time. The potlatch remains important in the lives of the people, because of both its historical significance and its contemporary relevance.

Booktalk

Through Indian Eyes: The Native Experience in Books for Children edited by Beverly Slapin and Doris Seale

If you have ever wondered how to evaluate the way Native Americans are portrayed in a particular children's book, Slapin and Seale's *Through Indian Eyes* is the place to start. First published in 1987 and most recently updated in 1992, this book contains reviews of more than a hundred children's books on Native Americans. The reviews, written from a native perspective, help the reader understand the kinds of subtle and not-so-subtle stereotypes that underpin some of the writing on native peoples. In addition to the reviews, the book provides the reader with a list of criteria to help evaluate other literature. The volume also includes essays by native writers such as Michael A. Dorris, Doris

Seale, and Joseph Bruchac, and a selection of poetry. A list of resources about native peoples, a bibliography of recommended books for children and an annotated bibliography of American Indian authors for young readers (originally published in 1973) round out the volume. An excellent reference tool, this book should be in every school library for frequent reference by teachers, librarians, and parents.

Indians of North America Series
Chelsea House Publishers

The Indians of North America series fills a gap in the literature on Native Americans by providing a comprehensive look at more than fifty Native American tribes from different areas of North America. Included are the Navajo, the Maya, and the Cherokee as well as lesser known tribes such as the Quapaws, the Catawbas, and the Tarahumara. A stated goal of the series is "to give all Americans a greater comprehension of the issues and conflicts involving American Indians today." Written for a young adult audience (age ten and up), each book discusses traditional practices in cultural context. The books also address the specific relationship each tribe has had with the federal government. Among the authors are historians, anthropologists, and other scholars. Each book is illustrated with maps and modern and historic photographs. All contain glossaries and annotated bibliographies.

For a study of the peoples of the Northwest Coast, two books in the series are excellent for research: *The Kwakiutl* by Stanley Walens and *The Coast Salish Peoples* by Frank W. Porter III. Used together, the books provide a sense of some of the different issues facing tribal groups in similar environments.

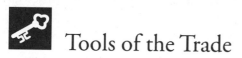 Tools of the Trade

Using a Lending Artifact Kit

For the Northwest Coast study, the analysis of authentic artifacts was an integral part of the learning experience. While assembling an artifact collection to use for a study is beyond the budget of most schools, cultural institutions may have lending kits that can be borrowed for a week to a month for a relatively modest fee. These kits may include visual materials, such as slide sets and videos; posters or display panels to decorate the classroom; artifacts or specimens for students to examine and analyze; raw materials from which the artifacts were made; printed materials for student use; and a teacher's guide.

While lending kits have been available from some institutions for a long time, some have been eliminated because of the expense of developing and maintaining collections that get such heavy use. In the last few years, however, the availability of kits has been on the rise, as other cultural institutions have turned to lending kits as a way of expanding their reach into schools. What does this mean to you, the teacher? It may mean that places from which you borrowed materials in the past have eliminated their lending program, while places you've contacted unsuccessfully before may now have new programs, or may be developing them. It may also mean that the kinds of kits you find available today differ substantially from ones you may have borrowed in the past, in terms of content as well as design. Newer kits may be more durable, but well-worn favorites also have their appeal.

While local institutions may have such kits available for rental, do not limit your search to only these sources. Some institutions lend their kits nationally, while others restrict the loans to schools within the state.

How do you find these kits? In the past, recommendations from colleagues and brochures mailed to teachers were the main sources. Telephone and mail were the methods used to contact the institutions and to learn what was available and at what charge. Today, almost every major cultural institution offering lending kits has mounted a site on the World Wide Web.

There are several ways to approach your search through the Internet. You can begin by looking at the sites of major cultural institutions in your state and seeing what they have available. You can also search by subject (for example, "Kwakiutl") and find sites that way. Teacher magazines are another source of information about kits. A recent article in a teacher publication that mentioned one of the lending kits available from the Boston Children's Museum, for example, led to a dramatic increase in requests for the kit. Within a few weeks of the article's publication, the kits were booked for the entire year.

It is important to look for lending kits early and make your bookings far in advance. Some of the kits are very popular or are booked year after year by the same teachers. Since the number of each kit available is usually quite restricted, many kits are in very heavy demand. Consider sharing a kit with a colleague on your grade level. Even if it would be ideal to have the kit in your room for the entire length of your study, having it for half a day or for several consecutive days would be better than not having the materials at all.

Remember also that while the focus here is on artifacts to supplement the teaching of history, the institutions you will find may also have wonderful science kits. Once you've experienced the rewards of teaching with collections of objects in the classroom you may find many other ways to use objects for class-room enrichment.

Creating a Classroom Artifact Set

Consider the possibility of assembling your own artifact collection for your classroom. If you plan to stick with a topic for several years, investment in your own collection of teaching objects may be more cost-effective than renting kits year after year. Classroom collections need not be large, but the objects must be engaging enough to use in a variety of ways. Painted pottery with elaborate designs, for example, may be more useful than an unadorned vase. Students can analyze design elements, use the elements to create their own design motifs, and investigate the various images. Sculptural objects or pottery with sculpted facades can be used for mold making. By pressing self-hardening clay into the facade of a sculpted pot, for example, students can create molds to make partial replicas of important design features. You may want to make a full classroom set of replicas for the whole class to analyze.

Consider purchasing museum-quality replicas. Don't limit yourself to objects available locally. Good-quality objects are often available through museum catalogs. Here again, the proliferation of on-line sites means that you can locate items from distant institutions, with pricing and color photographs quickly available at your fingertips. Indigenous cultural centers may also have items available for purchase, as may small galleries. The Kwakiutl cultural center, part of the U'Mista Cultural Society, for example, once offered to put together a small collection of objects on the Kwakiutl tailor-made to fit a par-ticular curriculum. At a local conference on Amazonian people, a colleague met a member of an upstate Mohawk tribal council who offered to make and sell authentic objects and to connect her to other members of his council who could offer a range of items.

Ideally, objects selected should be able to be handled frequently by stu-dents; in other words, durability is a consideration. But don't eliminate the pos-sibility of using breakable items, such as pottery. Students should be instructed to handle objects appropriately, and the small nicks and chips that may occur over years of use will not necessarily detract from the object's usefulness.

Think about assembling the raw materials that objects are made from. For the preparation of a teaching cart on pottery for the Mesoamerican Hall at the American Museum of Natural History, the educators who designed the cart assembled local raw materials such as clay from local soil (kept in a double plastic bag), slip (for the surface decoration), pigments (from commercial distributors), and an ear of dried corn (because the design motif on one of the pots incorporated a corn motif). Often visitors are as interested in the raw materials as they are in the finished product, and your students may react in the same way. For children who have never felt unprocessed clay, squishing it between their fingers, discussing how it is turned into a usable material is an important part of understanding how an object was made. Be creative in your quest for raw materials. Local plant stores, seed catalogs, craft stores and catalogs, children's catalogs, specialty food stores, and traveling friends, colleagues, and relatives can all be sources of raw materials. Remember also that raw materials are often much cheaper than the finished product. While they may or may not be actually usable by your students, they are still worth examining and discussing.

Researching On-Line

There are several interesting Web sites related to the Kwakiutl. The U'Mista Cultural Society site contains information about current issues, research, and programs, as well as some historical information about the Kwakiutl. Descriptions of a traditional big house and ceremonies can be used for classroom research. While there is not much bibliographic material on line, the Society will provide an extensive bibliography on request. Included in the bibliography are books for children, including primers Kwakiutl children use to learn about their own culture, language tapes, art books, academic books aimed at a scholarly audience, postcards, and posters.

A site mounted by Bruce Hallman has been recognized by Netguide magazine, *Alive!* and InfoSeek Select as an excellent site for Kwakiutl history. Listed on a wide variety of Web pages including NativeWeb, Karen Strom's Native American Web page, Hallman's site provides maps, historical photographs and documents, explorer's reports, and a number of traditional recipes for preparing salmon, halibut, and other foods important to the Kwakiutl.

For information about other Native American sites consult the pages listed below. In addition to topics such as history, art, and indigenous people's organizations, Karen Strom's Web site includes links to photographic archives, electronic texts, and on-line course materials.

For Northwest Coast resources, check the following:

U'Mista Cultural Society:
   http://www.schoolnet.ca/ext/aboriginal/umista1/index.html
Bruce Hallman's Kwakiutl pages: http://ftp.netgate.net/~bruce

For general Native American resources, try these Web sites:

NativeWeb: http://www.nativeweb.org/
Karen Strom's index of Native American resources:
   http://hanksville.phast.umass.edu/misc/NAresources.html

CHAPTER FIVE

Long Ago: Imagining the Pilgrims

"Amy has the quissies," announced Sara one morning during our class meeting. "I spoke to her on the phone last night and she told me that she had been casting and scouring all day."

It is winter and we are all sick. Rare is the day that all my students are in school. Flu and stomach viruses are rampaging among us. All day long I hear the rattle of cough drop boxes. Bleary-eyed, I drag myself to school, sniffling and coughing along with the best of them. How appropriate it seems to be learning about the Pilgrims and their harsh first winter in the New World, when illness caused so many deaths. The quissies, we learn, was a seventeenth-century expression for upset stomachs. From a first-hand account we read that some Mayflower passengers "found great mussels, and very fat and full of sea-pearl, but we could not eat them, for they made us all sick that did eat, as well sailors as passengers. They caused to cast and scour"—to vomit and have diarrhea, my students gleefully discover.

Bodily functions are so beloved by children; even the most mature fourth grader can't avoid giggling when they come up in discussion. While I knew my students were enjoying our Pilgrim studies, it was hard for me to assess how well they were connecting to them as real people. For all I could tell these true stories were no different to them then the fairy tales we had studied earlier in the year. However, using language of the past to describe their present reassured me that they were seeing the Pilgrims as real people—people who got sick and threw up as we do today.

"Well," I say, "at least I know Amy will be back soon, as good as new. And if she ate bad mussels I'm sure, like the Pilgrims, she'll be more careful in the future!"

Many years ago, as I prepared to teach U.S. history for the first time to fourth graders, I was determined to help the children understand how long ago it had been since the first Europeans came to North America. Taking my life in my hands, I clambered on top of desks and wrapped brown paper all around my classroom, as high above the blackboard and bulletin boards as I could reach. The textbook I was using at the time indicated that the Vikings were the earliest Europeans to arrive, so I had diligently marked off centuries far enough back to include the time of the Vikings. On the first day of school I enthusiastically asked the students to place their own birthdays on this time line. Then, as we learned about the Vikings and others who had traveled to America, we added information about their journeys to the time line. Of course it was easy to see that the Vikings made their voyages a long time before our current day. They were over the blackboard in the front of the room, whereas the children's birthdays were all the way in the back. Throughout that year I earnestly had my students add to the time line, hopeful that they were gaining a better sense of chronology. But they seemed never to look at the chart or refer to it at all. We became busy, engrossed in the drama of the Revolution, the writing of the Constitution, the horrors of the Civil War. How long ago it all was did not seem particularly important. In subsequent years, disappointed, I finally dispensed with the time line. Convinced that it just didn't seem to make any difference, I decided that my students simply were not developmentally ready for such an understanding about time. Better to accept that children of this age have only a very simple grasp of time, able to understand only that some events occurred long ago and that certain events had happened before others. That was good enough for me. My goals were not about my students' understanding the concept of time, after all, but about their learning about the past so they could better understand the present.

Years later, the idea of time came up again during a unit on Native Americans of the Southwest, as my students struggled to separate aspects of Anasazi and Pueblo life. The Anasazi were people who created and abandoned remarkable cliff dwellings in the Southwest between the eighth and fifteenth centuries, whereas the Pueblo are a contemporary Native American people, possibly related to the Anasazi. My class spent a great deal of time immersed in Anasazi life, synthesizing their knowledge through researching building construction, early farming, and pottery. However, when we turned our attention to the Pueblo of today, my students struggled to see the difference. For my New York City youngsters, the Pueblo people of the Southwest seemed very distant and different. Comments during class discussions made me realize that many children had no sense of how much further back in time the Anasazi were from the Pueblo of this century. After all, they both did pottery, used building methods that appeared similar to my urban students, and ate similar foods. To address this muddle, I had my students do a time line on the Anasazi and Pueblo people. It began in the seventh century, when the early Anasazi constructed pit dwellings on top of mesas; moved on to the eleventh century, when they created multiroom structures within cliffs and canyons, such as those at Mesa Verde and Chaco Canyon; then on to the later period, when they abruptly abandoned these places; to the nineteenth century, when Native Americans were "removed" by the U.S. government to reservations; and up to the present. Creating a visual image of time helped my students better recognize the differences between the ancient Anasazi and the Pueblo of today.

When I finally abandoned the U.S. history textbook and with it a chronological approach to teaching history, I also lowered the emphasis on time. No longer was I asking my students to memorize dates, to be able to tell me when the Boston Tea Party was or the Battle of Lexington. Of course, my students had some idea that certain aspects of our studies took place longer ago than others. When they seemed confused, I interceded, as I had with the Pueblo time line. However, I did not build the curriculum around a chronological sequence, nor did I focus lessons around the issue of time. No doubt part of my aversion stemmed from my own unpleasant memories of attempting to memorize dates for a test only to forget them shortly thereafter. However, it was also due to my observation of fourth graders over the years, as I watched them struggle to make sense of time. Just how long ago events took place just didn't seem as important as other things I hoped they would learn. An overemphasis on time, I was afraid, would narrow their interest and close down their openness to learning about a culture far away and different from their own.

For several years I was able to avoid dealing much with chronology because the fourth-grade curriculum emphasized oral history, non-Western ways of keeping history, and recent history. However, with the introduction of a new fourth-grade social studies unit on American colonization I had to grapple once more with the issue of chronology.

The Pilgrim unit came about when my colleagues and I were urged to include more U.S. history in our social studies curriculum. We decided to follow up our immigration unit with one on the early English colonists because they too had been immigrants. Coincidentally, I happened to be in the school office one day when a representative from Plimoth Plantation, a living history museum in Massachusetts that recreates the original Pilgrim settlement, came in. He mentioned that the Mayflower Society of New York sponsored a visit by a Plimoth interpreter to any interested schools in the city. His enthusiasm for Plimoth Plantation and their interpreters was infectious, and I was fascinated by the idea that they made it as authentic as possible. While not yet teaching the new unit on the colonial period, I decided to take advantage of the opportunity anyway, hopeful that it would enrich the children's thinking about the past.

The Plimoth visitor came to my class on May 9, 1996. For him, however, it was 1627. He was not a Pilgrim, but a member of the settlement from London who had come to the New World to make his fortune rather than to seek religious freedom. By this point in the year, my students had spent a great deal of time considering what history was. In preparation for the Plimoth visitor, I had asked the children to come up with questions connected to their own studies that year of immigration, Native Americans, and government. The visit was an even greater success than I could have hoped for. The children, highly skeptical at the beginning of the day ("We aren't studying the Pilgrims, so why do we have to listen to him?"), were starry-eyed by the end. The interpreter stayed in character all day and answered the children's prepared questions in great detail as well as the many others that tumbled out throughout the day.

My imagination stimulated, I made a visit to Plimoth Plantation. I was extremely impressed with the research done to make the settlement appear as accurate as possible. Somehow this setting was real, yet long ago. On a cold day I found men outside building a fence, women heading to the communal oven to bake, others in their homes praying and preparing food. Chatting with these well-prepared actors was a revelation. These were not the Pilgrims of my childhood. I saw no turkeys, and many of the settlers told me that they weren't there for religious freedom at all, but to make their fortunes. Moving beyond the plantation, I came to Hobbamock's Homesite, an Indian settlement. The guides there were Native Americans dressed in seventeenth-century attire who, unlike the plantation interpreters, spoke as people today describing the past. Again the truth came up against my memories. The Wampanoag were a sophisticated people, nothing like the simplistic characters I recalled from childhood Thanksgiving tales.

I began reading voraciously about the Pilgrims. I found *Mourt's Relation,* a journal written by a member of the settlement and published only a few years after the *Mayflower* first arrived, and William Bradford's memoir, *Of Plymouth Plantation.* I discovered a wonderful trove of children's books, the most recent ones carefully researched to provide as authentic a view of these mythologized people as possible.

For the next year I continued to collect and read materials about the Pilgrims, and I returned to Plimoth Plantation. As I taught my immigration unit that year I considered how the Pilgrims were immigrants too. How might I connect my students' experience in oral history to immigrants from so long ago? How was I going to help my students see these people as real, not figures of myth? How was I going to help my students deal with the concept of time?

As I learned more and thought more about the subject, I realized that the answer was in imaginative thinking. My imagination had been stimulated by the Plimoth interpreters acting as settlers of long ago. Somehow I wanted to stimulate my students' imaginations in the same way. Having them travel back in time in their imaginations, to envision these long-ago people as real would be the key, I felt, for a successful learning experience.

I prepared for the unit by collecting as many books as I could find, developing a framework, thinking about specific activities, and, most important, keeping a stance of openness. This was uncharted territory for me. Just as the

Pilgrims had come to Cape Cod with certain expectations and preparations—John Smith's map of the area, their knowledge of previous travelers to the New World, tools and supplies, their faith and optimism—so I began my Pilgrim unit full of theories, ideas, plans, materials, and enthusiasm. Yet also like the Pilgrims I had to be flexible—ready for the unexpected, ready to change direction and focus in response to my students' needs—just as the settlers had had to deal with unexpected weather and illness. I didn't know if my students would be able to read excerpts from *Mourt's Relation* as I had planned any more than the Pilgrims could count on a good harvest. I didn't know if my students could view people of so long ago as real any more than the Pilgrims could consider the Native Americans as people like themselves. I knew, however, that my students enjoyed learning and had vivid imaginations—imaginations that I hoped would bring them into this historical period.

In the end, the unit included the following parts:

- Preparing to travel back in time.
- Getting to know the Pilgrims. The students would uncover prior knowledge by reading, annotating, and taking notes from primary and secondary sources, and would use this information to construct a time line.
- A Pilgrim picture book project. Students would study commercially published books on the Pilgrims and then work with a variety of sources within a writing workshop environment to create an original storybook.
- A Wampanoag's point of view. We would look at the meeting of the Pilgrims and the Wampanoag from the Native American perspective.
- Time travel to Plymouth, Massachusetts. As the culminating event of the unit, the entire fourth grade would make an overnight trip to Plimoth Plantation.

My Goals

I had several goals in mind with this unit, including the following:

- With the Pilgrims, my students were looking at history of the more traditional sort. This was the kind of history that was included in textbooks, that was traditionally considered significant, "important." I hoped that our close look at this sort of history would merge with my students' experience with oral history to deepen their own personal definitions of just what history is.
- The focus on primary and secondary sources would, I hope, help my students see themselves as interpreting material the way real historians do.

- Studying a range of materials as we tried to come up with a view of the Pilgrim experience I hoped would strengthen my students' ability to question texts. They would be able to see that the materials were written by real people with varying points of view.
- Considering the Pilgrims as early immigrants to North America and connecting them to our earlier work with immigrants today would help my students generalize about immigration in different time periods.
- Reading primary sources would help make the Pilgrims and their experiences seem real to my students.
- I hoped my students would recognize the paradox of the Pilgrims wanting religious freedom while being unable to understand the religious beliefs of the Native Americans they encountered.
- My students would understand the purpose of history: through connecting the Pilgrims' immigration experiences with those of contemporary immigrants, they would see how learning about the past helps us better understand the present.

Preparing to Travel Back in Time

I thought a great deal about how I would approach the issue of time with my students. I didn't want them to become bogged down in dates; however, I did believe that they had to get a sense that the Pilgrims' experience in America was a long time ago. I decided to challenge the children to write a letter to people in the future, to those who would be researching them just as my students were going to be researching the long-ago Pilgrims. My students' letters would be first-person accounts—the sort of documents they would be reading when they began to do their Pilgrim research. Together we decided that the letters would be addressed to people 377 years in the future, the same distance in time that they would experience as they read about the Pilgrims (1997 minus 1620, the year the *Mayflower* set sail). Adding 377 to 1997, my students calculated, brought them to the year 2374. My students loved the specificity of that number. We discussed the sorts of information they would want to gather as they researched the Pilgrims and would need to include in their letters to the future. The children came up with the following subjects to include in their letters:

Technology	Clothing/fashion
Living	Leisure time activities (computers, TV, videos,
Pets	sports, games)
Food	Transportation
Schooling/education	Work

The list was full of what interests today's students. I pointed out that other things, such as religion, were more important to the Pilgrims and might also be of interest to our readers of the future. With that hint, they added religion to the list.

The letters my students wrote to the people of 2374 were rich with my students' interests as well as their genuine efforts to inform their readers of the future about late-twentieth-century life. In several cases they recognized that what was well known today might not be well known in the future.

Aly wrote, "My favorite sport is basket ball. That is when two groups take a ball and try to get it in a hoop."

Charles wrote, "My name is Charles and I am 10 years old. I attend the Dalton School, a place where you learn things."

Bobby wrote, "We write on paper with a pen or a marker or a pencil. Our fashion is blue jeans and a blue shirt usually. Our pets are fish, dogs, guinea pigs, frogs, and cats."

Elizabeth wrote, "I am nine and in a few weeks I will be ten. I live in an apartment in a building. A building is a big brick structure. An apartment is a small part of a building."

Ariel informed her future readers that "the fashion now is dark blue jeans and dark glasses."

Asked, at the end of our Pilgrim unit, how the Letters to the Future activity had helped them in their study of long-ago people, some of my students honestly told me it had not helped them.

Chris forthrightly wrote, "I really learned nothing because it had nothing to do with what we were doing." This sentiment was echoed by several of his peers.

Alie had mixed reactions, writing that the activity "wasn't as success[ful] as it could be . . . but it was to warm us up."

However, others were stimulated by the activity. Bobby felt it was a good idea because "in the year 3000 people will look back at our letters if they are still around and say, 'So this is what the kids in the year 1997 did.'"

Amanda felt that "in 377 years we will become history and things will be strange to people 377 years forward."

For David, the activity helped him to understand that "the Pilgrims didn't write their things for historical references," while Ariel realized that "books are not always right."

The range of understanding that resulted with the Letter to the Future activity has me uncertain whether I would do it again. Some children saw no point to it at all. They felt it was about the future, not the past. For them learning was knowledge, especially factual knowledge, and this activity did not provide them with new facts to know. However, other children understood learning to be a more intellectual process, and they could look back at this activity at the end of the Pilgrim unit and see how it had helped them to look at the past from a broader perspective. Whether I do the activity again or not will depend on the class. If I have a group of children who I think will appreciate the intellectual challenge, I will use it. If the group appears to have a more factual orientation, I will probably try a different activity.

Getting to Know the Pilgrims

It was finally time to get started with our study of the Pilgrims. I began by saying to my students, "You are going to be serious historians, finding out about the real Pilgrims behind the myth. The Pilgrims were immigrants who had reasons for coming to America similar to those people still have today. You already know so much about contemporary immigration because of your oral history projects. Remember your great questions and how you crafted the resulting interview into picture books? Now you are going to attempt to do something similar with a real person from 377 years ago. Since the Pilgrims aren't here to interview, you will have to get your information some other way. Learning ways to do that will be a major part of your work in this assignment. In the process, you will become a Pilgrim expert, ready to travel back in time to visit Plimoth Plantation itself!"

Enthusiastically, the children began to tell me all they already knew about the Pilgrims. "Hold on a minute!" I laughed. "Let me get this down on paper!" On a large piece of chart paper I wrote down all they told me. This chart would be posted for us to refer to throughout the unit. As the children got deeper into their research they were able to identify the inaccuracies of their previous knowledge.

Here is what we wrote:

What We Already Know About the Pilgrims
They came on a boat called the *Mayflower*.
They had the first Thanksgiving.
They came with rifles.
They came to America so they could practice their religion.
Their boat was stinky, smelly, overcrowded, and the food was despicable.
They fought the Indians.
The Indians helped them build houses and grow food.
A lot of Pilgrims died of smallpox.

A lot of Pilgrims froze to death over the winter.
They came 377 years ago.
They first arrived at what is now Plymouth.
They were immigrants.
They didn't all come from England.
Pocahontas had to do with the Pilgrims.
It took them a long time to adapt to the American environment.
During the winter they had trouble getting food.

I asked my students where they had gotten this information and was told it was from movies, books, the barrage of information around Thanksgiving, special storytellers and school assemblies, and museums.

A Pilgrim Time Line

To help my students begin their trip back in time, I asked them to create a time line, focusing specifically on events involving the Pilgrims. Often a study of American colonization begins with a close look at Europe of the time: the living conditions and politics that made people want to leave. However, I wanted us to look at the Pilgrims as we had our immigration oral history subjects, and I felt that focusing on issues of seventeenth-century Europe would draw my students' attention away from our primary topic: the Pilgrims' move to North America. I also wanted our initial activity to give my students experience and help them develop skills in extracting information from difficult texts, so that they would acquire the tools they would need to evaluate primary and secondary sources.

I gave the children a packet containing an essay on the Pilgrims written for children by the Plimoth Plantation staff, excerpts from *Mourt's Relation,* and a passenger list of the *Mayflower.*

Secondary Source Reading

We began with the essay written by the staff of Plimoth Plantation for classroom use. This was a secondary source that provided a chronological overview of the Pilgrim experience.

I introduced the activity by describing how I alter my own ways of reading depending on my purpose. When I read a novel like *Charlotte's Web,* for example, my stance is different from when I read a piece of nonfiction to get information. I further explained that when reading a novel I like to immerse myself in the world created by the author. While I need to pick up certain information from my reading, say that Charlotte is a spider and that Wilbur is young and naive, mostly I allow myself to be drawn along by the emotional experience of the book. Louise Rosenblatt (1991) terms this the aesthetic experience of reading. When reading material about the Pilgrims, however, I have a different way of reading. In this case I am looking for information: when they lived, why they came, what their lives were like. The emotional component is less important. Rosenblatt terms this the efferent stance of reading.

I modeled how I would approach such a text. I gave the children copies of the essay and then I read aloud as they followed along. Rather then just jumping in at the beginning I demonstrated how I would skim through the whole text, note the subheadings, and see what it contained before beginning to read. I explained that I might choose not to read all of it, but only the parts that were likely to provide the information I was seeking. While the Pilgrim experience may be presented as a story, collecting information from that story does not necessarily mean that one must read it in a linear fashion, as one usually does for a story.

Next, I modeled my reading of the first section. I showed how I would read and reread to understand the material, how I might use a dictionary to help me make better sense of the material. I demonstrated how I would highlight, underline, and circle parts of the text that were of particular interest to me. I demonstrated how I would jot significant material from the text down elsewhere as a way of extracting what I most wanted to know from the text.

The children paired off to read and paraphrase assigned sections of the essay for our time line. This was fascinating to watch. Most children needed days to truly make sense of their sections. It was a new experience for them to read and reread a small amount of text, to gain a complete knowledge of it, and then to paraphrase it in their own words. My students' lack of background knowledge as well as unfamiliarity with the vocabulary made this a very challenging experience for them.

Michael and Elizabeth had been given a section on how the Pilgrims' journey was funded. This was tough stuff. They were completely unfamiliar with many of the words and had no economic background to draw upon. Even dictionary definitions didn't suffice. Investors were an alien idea to them until I intervened and explained what they were. As I described the way the investors and the Pilgrims made up a group and what was meant by a "share," Michael's eyes lit up. "It's exactly like SimCity!" he exclaimed.

"What's SimCity?" I asked.

"A computer simulation where you have to create a city. They have stuff like investors and shares in it." With that, Michael dashed off, able to use his computer game skills to make sense of the seventeenth-century Pilgrims and their investors.

Spencer initially wanted to put every detail into his contribution to the class time line. He had a hard time determining what in his reading was most important for his needs and what he could ignore. After I talked with him about this, he returned sometime later with the opposite problem: he had highlighted a few minor details of the text, leaving out important pieces of information. Gingerly, I tried to help him achieve a more balanced approach. "You tried your best, and I see what you tried to do here," I told him. "This is a very hard thing to do, to know what is too much and what is too little." Fortunately, Spencer took my suggestions with good humor and went off to search deeper for information on the Pilgrims.

Once all the children had finished reading and paraphrasing their sections they presented the results to the class. This provided the whole class with an overview of the Pilgrim experience. After the presentations they posted their summaries on the back bulletin board—where we were creating our time line of the Pilgrim experience.

At the end of the Pilgrim unit I was unexpectedly delighted to read in their self-evaluations that most of the children had found this challenging reading of a secondary source a meaningful activity. I had worried that it was too hard for some of them and that I was going to put them off such reading for good. Fortunately, their comments at the end of the unit were quite the opposite: they looked back on this experience in a very positive manner.

Amanda felt it was a good experience because "you get a beginning flavor of the Pilgrims."

Elana felt that "It went great! We had to read a lot."

Spencer felt he "became an expert on one section and learned about the others."

Bobby felt that he had "learned that you don't have to highlight the whole piece of writing to get the main idea."

The combination of learning many new facts along with new methods for reading made all the students feel that they had completed the activity successfully.

Primary Source Reading

We then moved on to read excerpts from *Mourt's Relation.* On the basis of my observations of their difficulties with the Plimoth Plantation essay, I decided that the best way to read this primary source material would be in study groups. I knew that the children would not be able to rely on dictionaries to make sense of the reading because words are often used differently in *Mourt's Relation* from the way they are used today. I hoped that a larger group would enable them together to make meaning out of a very old text.

To model the workings of a study group, I created one consisting of a learning specialist, a young assistant teacher, and myself. I asked the children to watch us work together for twenty minutes and write down all the strategies they saw us use to make meaning out of the text. It was a strange experience indeed, having my students watch me struggle through a text. It was rather like being on stage! After twenty minutes the three of us stopped, and the children described the strategies they had seen us use, some of which we weren't even aware of. I listed the strategies on a class chart:

Reading Pilgrim Primary Sources
Study Group Strategies

1. One person reads aloud a paragraph and others follow along.
2. When you don't know a word, stop and discuss it. Use prior knowledge and context clues to figure it out. (Avoid dictionaries because the word may be used differently from the way we use it today.)
3. Take notes, annotate, underline, and highlight.
4. Draw pictures and diagrams to help you understand.
5. Politely interrupt the reader if you don't understand. Figure it out as a group before reading further.
6. Check that everyone understands before going on.
7. Need to include all members of the group.
8. Take turns.
9. Reread and read ahead. Sometimes a word that you don't understand will be used again in a way that will make sense the second time.
10. Use the glossary to help figure out words.

The next day the children began their own group readings of selections from *Mourt's Relation*. I moved around the room observing them at work. All were taking the task very seriously and told me that it was easier to read than the Plimoth essay. They made use of the footnotes and tussled with both unfamiliar words and familiar words used in unfamiliar ways.

Once they had completed the readings I asked the children each to select one quote from the selections that they would illustrate. As they began I suddenly realized that they would have to rely on secondary sources for the illustrations. Few contemporary pictures of Pilgrim life exist; only one portrait of a Pilgrim existed, that of Edward Winslow.

The many carefully researched picture books on the Pilgrims ended up being our most helpful resources for the pictures. Before each work period I presented one or two books to the children, and we discussed how the illustrators had done their research. We also improved our understanding of why *Mourt's Relation* was a primary source while the various picture books were secondary sources. The children's final illustrations were posted below our Pilgrim time line along with facsimiles of relevant documents, such as a *Mayflower* passenger list and an early map of Cape Cod.

In their final self-evaluations the children indicated that they felt they had learned a great deal from this activity. Some wrote that they learned especially about working in groups, while others noted that they had learned about reading difficult materials. Ariel wrote that she "learned that I had to read the paragraph over and over to really get the main idea of it," while Bobby learned "the importance of underlining."

Others felt that they learned more about the importance of sources. Chris "learned what research you have to do for pictures."

Some were most struck by the additional facts they picked up from the readings, such as Spencer, who learned that "the Pilgrims had a very strong view about God and Indians," and David, who was struck by "the time when the Pilgrims took corn from an [Indian] graveyard."

As with the previous activity, the children came away with a heightened awareness of how to read difficult material for information as well as a richer personal data base of factual knowledge about the Pilgrims.

Historical Fiction

One of my students introduced me to *A Journey to the New World: The Diary of Remember Patience Whipple*, Kathryn Lasky's fictionalized account of the *Mayflower* experience. The book is written in the form of a diary by Remember, an imaginary *Mayflower* passenger. I had been reluctant to use historical fiction because I worried that the children might have trouble distinguishing fact from fiction.

However, sitting on the subway one afternoon after the project had started, I began reading Lasky's book and quickly realized that her book was carefully researched and that much of her information was taken from *Mourt's Relation*. Since my students had direct experience with *Mourt's Relation* it seemed that

Lasky's story might actually help them to see how one could use primary sources in a fictional account of a real event. Additionally, Lasky's characters were well formed and her narrator was a child my students could relate to. I decided to read the book aloud and have my students note the fictional and factual information as we went along. This proved to be a very successful activity. The children and I continually noted where Lasky had gleaned information from primary sources. Often I stopped reading so that we could page through *Mourt's Relation* to find the exact source of her writing. Toward the end of the book Lasky has Remember meet Native Americans. We looked closely at the description of Samoset's entrance into the village in *Mourt's Relation* and saw how Lasky fictionalized that account. (We were somewhat skeptical as to whether a 1621 Pilgrim girl would have interacted with Native Americans as does Lasky's heroine.)

Asked his opinion of the Lasky book, David wrote, "I like *A Journey to the New World* even though it is my second time reading it. It is like *Charlotte's Web:* you can never stop getting more things out of it."

"*A Journey to the New World* is very good," concluded Chris. "The writer even with a fictional character finds ways to capture the facts."

Alie wrote, "I think *A Journey to the New World* is a book that you wouldn't want to read, but it is a really good book so never judge a book by its cover. I think *Mourt's Relation* is like *A Journey to the New World* because both are letters and they both are explaining what is happening."

Lasky's book provided my students with a way to think of the Pilgrims as people like themselves. They were now ready to begin their own project, an imaginary interview with an immigrant of 1620.

A Pilgrim Picture Book Project

My original idea was for the students to use their immigrant oral history project as a guide. With the earlier project they had become very sensitive to the delicate issues involved in telling someone else's story. In that case the subject was alive and accessible to them for research. In the case of the Pilgrims, they had a new challenge: to simulate the oral history experience with people unavailable for a face-to-face interview. How would they do it?

We began by considering questions. What would we want to ask these people of long ago? Immediately it became clear to all of us that the questions the children had created for their oral history interviews months earlier would work beautifully. Together we reviewed the list, omitting questions that were inappropriate, such as those about citizenship. What follows is the original list, annotated to indicate the questions that were changed or eliminated (the original list, as used in connection with the oral history unit, can be found in Chapter 3):

Oral History Questions

1. Why did you emigrate?
2. Where did you come from, and where did you go when you first arrived?
3. When did you come here?
4. Who came with you?
5. How did you get to America? Tell me about some of your experiences.
6. How long was your trip? Tell me about it.
7. What did you think America would be like? What was it actually like?
8. Tell about your family at the time of your emigration.
9. Did anyone who came with you speak English? Did you? How did you learn English? (We eliminated this item, since the Pilgrims were all English.)
10. What was your childhood like? (We also eliminated this question, since most of the subjects were children.)
11. What things did you bring with you? What was your most valued item, and did you bring it? Did you have to leave special things behind?
12. What was your lifestyle when you first came here? (We changed the word "lifestyle" to "environment." It was unlikely that the Pilgrims would speak of the Indians in terms of their "lifestyle.")
13. Compare something from your old country with something in this country.
14. What were your feelings when you left?
15. How did you feel when you first came here?
16. What did you miss from the country you came from?
17. What did you like about your new country? What did you dislike?
18. Did you meet people when you first came here? Are you still friends with any of them?
19. What was the first landmark you saw? Do you have any stories about it? (We discussed how a landmark for the Pilgrims would have to be natural as opposed to the more likely man-made ones of the immigrant subjects.)

(We eliminated the following three questions because the country did not yet exist.)

20. What year did you become a citizen? When and where?
21. What did you need to know to become a citizen?
22. What was it like to become a citizen?

Subject Selection

Once the questions had been determined, my students had to choose interview subjects. This turned out to be a more complicated process than I had envisioned. My students and I had been discussing the issue of subjects since the beginning of the unit. They knew that in the course of the unit they were going to create a book about a Pilgrim, and we discussed this project frequently as we learned more. As I read the Lasky book to them we tried to notice when she was staying close to the facts in *Mourt's Relation* and when she was using her imagination to make something more exciting. We talked a lot about the differences between writing about an imaginary character as Lasky did and writing from the point of view of a real person from the past. When at one point I asked the class whether they wanted to take the voice of an imaginary person or a real one they all said they want to write as a real person.

Finally the day came when the class was ready to select subjects. Immediately we ran into trouble. Since so many *Mayflower* passengers died the first winter, I warned my students to be sure to select someone who survived. I realized too late this was not an easy task. Elana went off to the library to see what she could find about the passenger she had chosen and came back some time later with little to show for her efforts. Meanwhile, I was working with Michael, who was insistent on researching his subject's life in depth and asking for my help in finding resources. I had none. I quickly discovered that my carefully created classroom library of books on the Pilgrims had nothing on the man he had selected. In fact, the books had little on individual settlers. Most gave general information about the Pilgrim experience, which I had thought would be adequate. Clearly I was wrong. I was in a panic because it had not occurred to me that the children would want specific information on real people. Somehow I had thought that they could generalize from all the material we had already read about the Pilgrims, including the Plimoth Plantation essay and the *Mourt's Relation* excerpts. But my students wanted details, not vague generalizations. And they were quite right. If they were going to create a picture book about a real seventeenth-century English immigrant they had to make it as real as they had their oral history picture books.

That night I reflected on the events of the day. I had gone into the project certain that the children could use their imaginations to create stories about real people. Somehow that had seemed to me more authentic than making up both people and stories. Yet I had been so concerned that my students kept in mind that the Pilgrims were real people that I had lost sight of how hard, if not impossible, it would be to find details of these people's lives. I made a 180-degree turn in my thinking as I came to the realization that creating composite imaginary subjects would probably provide my students with a way to learn more without the frustration that researching a real person would cause. With an imaginary person, they would be free to take information from different sources without fear that they were being untrue to their subject.

The next day I had Elana and Michael explain their problems to the class. I then told the group of my new way of thinking, suggesting that instead of attempting to use real people as subjects they create composite characters. These characters could have names that were combinations of different actual Pilgrims' names, lives that were composites of different actual Pilgrims' lives.

Most of the children agreed that this would work much better than attempting to seek out information on less well known *Mayflower* passengers. It had become as clear to them as it had to me that there simply wasn't enough primary source material to create, honestly and realistically, an imaginary interview with a real *Mayflower* passenger. Two boys had become intrigued by William Bradford, however, and chose to write about him, while the rest of the children elected to create imaginary subjects. With the Plimoth Plantation essay, the *Mayflower* passenger list, several selections from *Mourt's Relation,* our time line, and the classroom library of Plimoth books, they were able to research and create compelling, realistic subjects.

They began with names. Several came up with names that simply sounded "nice." I challenged them to prove to me that these nice-sounding names were typical of *Mayflower* passengers. This they did by showing me these names in the primary sources we had. Often they combined first and last names from different *Mayflower* passengers. In one case this caused trouble: one child named his subject John Bradford, combining William Bradford's last name with John Allerton's first name. Later on, one of the boys researching the real William Bradford complained that his classmate couldn't use the name John Bradford, because that was the actual name of William Bradford's son. I tried to settle the dispute by noting that communities often have two people with the same name. In our class, for example, we had two Michaels. That quickly resolved the issue, and so we had John Bradford, the imaginary *Mayflower* passenger, and John Bradford, the real son of Governor Bradford.

Once they had decided on a name, the students' next task was to decide if the subject was a Protestant (Pilgrim) or a member of the Church of England. Not all of the *Mayflower* passengers were Pilgrims. Some came for economic, rather than religious, reasons. Deciding on birthdays and birthplaces was fun.

Using their math skills, many students determined that their subjects must have been born in Holland, where many Pilgrims had lived for over a decade before deciding to emigrate to the New World. One child decided that his subject was English and from London. Soon he was researching seventeenth-century London.

Interesting problems arose as children decided which family members came with their subjects and which stayed behind. Some boys were reluctant to include females in their group. They wanted to include small boys and no women whatsoever. It took several conversations and some research to convince them that small children would never have traveled without their mothers. One boy took the opposite tack, however, deciding to make his imaginary character female. I continually challenged the family groups my students created by insisting that they prove that such a family group had existed on the *Mayflower*. If they could prove that it did, I accepted the group. One child made his subject older so that he could avoid having women in his family group. Another began with eleven children and eventually brought the family size down to seven. Several children decided that their characters had left family members behind.

Imaginary Transcripts

Once the data sheets were complete the children began working on their imaginary transcripts. This was where their imaginations and research skills would intersect, at least so I hoped. For several weeks, the children worked in a writing workshop environment, looking at books and on the Internet for information that helped them to ground their transcripts in reality.

They worked hard to make their interview subject sound authentic and struggled to create compelling stories. The period vocabulary in Lasky's book, *Mourt's Relation,* and other sources inspired them, and the results were intriguing. Elana had discovered that "footing" meant "walking" and wrote that her subject's father had "footed around," while Courtney wrote, "It was so bad twasn't even funny." This resulted in a minilesson where we discussed how best to combine contemporary idioms with the Pilgrims vocabulary using the girls' examples. The enthusiasm for the old words was such that I started a list and the children added to it throughout the unit, often searching through the glossaries of various books for additions. Of course, words involving bodily functions were the most popular!

Pilgrim Imaginary Transcript
Good Words That We Have Discovered

Mother, Mam, ma	done (tired out)	dwelling
feather men	Father, Pa, sir	cast, spew, puke (vomit)
scours, quissies (diarrhea, upset stomach)	poppet (doll)	'twas (it was)
	'tis (it is)	folly (foolish)
	anon (immediately)	upgrown (grownup)
horrid	fearsome, dire (terrible)	want (lack)
fowl (animal)		
fetch (to get)	ado (commotion)	
morn (morning)	footing (walking)	

Our share sessions were opportunities for some children to get feedback on their work and others to get new ideas. Children challenged each other on style, anachronisms, and research. They also valued the ideas that they got from each other. I was amazed at their willingness to do substantive revision, often adding or eliminating whole paragraphs to make their transcripts sound as authentic as possible.

Storyboards

After completing their transcripts, the children followed the procedure of their oral history books and created storyboards. Some went through their transcripts first, highlighting sections they wished to include. The storyboards step got the children to start thinking more carefully about their illustrations—where they would get information to make them accurate, how much to put on a page. More revision occurred as they moved from the transcript to the storyboard.

Author's Notes and Sources

I required that every child include an author's note or introduction to explain the book. We had criticized Lasky's book for not including an author's note that clearly identified the protagonist as fictional, and for not providing a list of sources. My students recognized that they needed to identify their sources. After all, their fictional passengers and transcripts were based on real events and people of long ago. To be true to those seventeenth-century European immigrants, the children had to be sure that readers knew where the information had come from. Some included source information in an author's note, while others compiled bibliographies at the end of their books. All the books cited *Mourt's Relation* and at least one secondary source.

Courtney titled her book "What's to Become of Us?" and wrote in her author's note:

> This book is historical fiction. It is about a girl named Ellen Turner who has an eight year old brother named Steven, a four year old sister named Annabelle and, of course, a mother and father. Ellen Turner is a Pilgrim who boarded the Mayflower for religious freedom and even though you don't hear her say it, she is always wondering, "What is to become of us?"

Wrote David, in "Plymouth 2 Plymouth: Before and After the Pilgrim's Journey":

> We loosened from our study of recent immigration and into the vast sea of the Pilgrims many months ago. Our study goes back to 1534 when Henry the VIII established Anglicanism as the official religion of England to the late 18th century when the Pilgrims became acknowledged as America's forefathers. I have created a composite character, taking the last name of Issac Allerton [from the *Mayflower* passenger list] and using Francis, a popular boy's name during that time.

Charles wrote:

> Over the last couple of months my class embarked on a journey researching the Pilgrims of Plimoth. Our final assignment was to make a book on a Pilgrim who was really on the Mayflower! Everyone immediately debated over doing a composite character or a real person. Everyone except me and another colleague chose a composite character. I did not because William Bradford interested me. I shall waste no more of your precious time and hope you enjoy "Plimoth from Bradford's Point of View."

These introductions were all written after the rest of the books had been completed and gave my young authors an opportunity to reflect on their learning experience as well as providing me with yet another window into their learning process.

Illustrations

As with the oral history immigration books, the children used a range of media for their illustrations. Each child reviewed his or her earlier book and decided whether to reuse certain techniques or to use different ones. For the Pilgrim unit, the children used their knowledge from the earlier project and focused more on accuracy than on artistic technique. We studied picture books on the Pilgrims and noted how some illustrators had done a great deal of research to make their work as accurate as possible while others had drawn on general myths about the Pilgrims. By this time the children knew that the Pilgrims had not worn buckles on their shoes and did not wear only dark clothes, which often was the way they were depicted in older books. We found Kate Waters's books, of which *Sarah Morton's Day* is one, particularly helpful. Her books are photographic essays set at Plimoth Plantation, carefully researched to show what Pilgrim life looked like. In addition to picture books, we looked at contemporary art of the time, such as seventeenth-century portrait and landscapes, and furniture.

With this second illustrated book project, the children were often more influenced by each other than by professional illustrators. Ariel and Chris had created striking double-page layouts in their immigration books, and several children picked up this idea for their Pilgrim book. For their earlier book, a number of children had been inspired by commercial books and used borders around their text. For their book on the Pilgrims, many more children used borders, but this time they were inspired by their peers, not professional illustrators.

When we reached the illustration stage of the project I held frequent mini-lessons to celebrate the varying techniques and ideas at work. Alie proudly showed her illustration of the *Mayflower* voyage with a passenger spouting a cartoon bubble showing him counting out the sixty-six days of the journey. Michael beamed as the class admired his amusing sea life bounding beneath and around the *Mayflower;* before long sea life was popping up in other children's books as well. In one drawing, Chris drew men dressed in the red coats and tall hats of the guards he had seen at Buckingham Palace. He had been sure that all "old" English people were Redcoats. We talked about the American Revolution being over one hundred years after the *Mayflower* and then considered what the English immigrants would more likely have worn. Not red coats, it turned out!

In every case, the children made a conscious effort to have these books turn out even better than their oral history books had. Those who had created hasty drawings for their earlier books spent far more time on the art this time and were especially proud of their finished books. Others felt their Pilgrim books were more creative than their earlier ones because they had used more interesting ideas from their peers. All felt that they had done more research, which made their books artistically better.

Alie's Book

Alie was the youngest child in the class; she would be ten in June. Much as Alie loved learning, it didn't always love her back. Reading in particular had come slowly to Alie, so slowly that it was decided that she should repeat first grade. When Alie got wind of this, however, she was so upset that the decision was rescinded and Alie moved on to second grade with her original age group. Caring parents, tutors, and teachers over the next few years all helped Alie progress as a reader, and she came into fourth grade happy and pleased to be learning. Fortunately, her struggles with reading had never caused her to dislike learning. In fact, she loved being read to, loved to write, and was enthusiastic about all aspects of school. Her brother, whom she admired tremendously, had been in my class two years earlier, and Alie came into my classroom delighted to be there.

Alie decided that her Pilgrim subject would be male, modeled on her older brother. She had him travel on the *Mayflower* with his father and brother and checked the original passenger list to be sure such a family group had existed. However, she did have to make him older. I pointed out to her that a very young boy would have probably stayed with his mother. She made her character 15, old enough to be on his own, but young enough to still be childlike. The data sheet Alie developed for her character read as follows:

Subject's Name: Edward Milton
Religion: Protestant
Birthplace: Scrooby, England
Birthdate: 2/19/1604
Age at time of immigration: 15 years
Traveled to North America: With his brother and dad.
With family (list family members, who came, who stayed behind)
   John Milton, brother, 20 years
   William Milton, father
   Mary Milton, mother, stayed
   Frances Milton, baby, stayed with mom

Alie's Imaginary Transcript: During our Pilgrim periods Alie worked with a ferocious intensity. I would look over and see her huddled over her paper, writing with furious concentration. She told me later that while she was writing, "I pretended I was my Pilgrim" back in 1621 America. Periodically, she would come to me to read some of what she had written. She also enjoyed reading sections to the class during our share sessions.

I asked the children to add a paragraph about their Pilgrim work in their weekly journal letters to me. In one of these letters Alie wrote, "I was going to make my guy's brother always flirting with girls (like Chris!) so he would wander off and meet an Indian and they would be best friends. Then he finds out he's a girl, but he does not care. But that got out of hand so I forgot it." Later Alie revived this idea by writing an afterword to her book where she noted that Edward married a Native American. When I read this I told her I wasn't sure this ever happened and she should check to see if it was a possibility. She searched through several books, then decided that it probably was unrealistic and changed the wife to an English girl. When reflecting back, Alie felt that this was an important revision. The wife, she wrote, "couldn't be Indian because they wouldn't have had a relationship and you couldn't put anything in that couldn't really have happened."

Alie worked hard to integrate all she had learned about the Pilgrims' reasons for coming to America along with further details of their life in Holland. In her transcript, she wrote, "My father was worried because he was a cobbler and he did not get enough money and there was a war coming so my father, my brother, and me left to the New World and left my sister and mother behind."

Along with others, Alie was particularly intrigued by the son of Francis Billington who, according to *Mourt's Relation,* got ahold of some gunpowder and a gun and, while on the *Mayflower,* "shot her off in the cabin" and started a fire, "yet, by God's mercy, no harm done." In *Mourt's Relation* there is also an account of a trip to a Native American village in search of a lost boy. I suggested to Alie that she might want to put that into her transcript as well. Eventually, Alie wrote:

I came in the Mayflower and I met a boy who became my best friend. His name was John Billington. He almost blew up the Mayflower. That's why I like him. He reminds me of my best friend who stayed behind who always got in trouble. He also ran away once. When I found out that I volunteered to be in the search party. Late at night we set off to Nauset where they

> said he was. We arrived and they delivered us him with beads all over
> and so we left and he said, "I have so many stories to tell you."

Alie tried to balance her own family experiences with what she learned about the English families. At first she wanted her subject to complain about his little sister. However, I pointed out that someone that long ago might not feel the way older siblings today feel about younger siblings. Since she was interested in writing about her character's flirtatiousness I also suggested that it might have been a reason for their immigration since some books indicated that the Pilgrims in Holland worried that they would become too assimilated into Dutch society. Alie wrote:

> My sister Frances was two and always would get in my way, but I hardly cared. Now she is eight and she is not that bad, but coming to the New World with me and my older brother John who is the reason we left to the New World. He would always be attracted to the Dutch girls. So he made us leave which made me mad because I was very fond of a Dutch girl myself.

Alie tended to wax poetic and go off into long, lyrical stories. However, I wanted to be sure that she included historical information as well. She welcomed my suggestions and enjoyed researching aspects of Pilgrim life more deeply. Balancing her desire to create a fully realized character with a need to be historically accurate was a challenge she took on with great enthusiasm.

Alie's Storyboard: Alie used most of her transcript in composing her storyboard. With my help she also reorganized her work. At first she simply wrote the story in the order of her transcript questions. I pointed out to her that this made the chronology unclear, as the transcript moved back and forth in time, from the *Mayflower* journey, back to Holland, forward to the New World, and then back to the *Mayflower.* Together we reorganized her pages to make the narrative more coherent. She also eliminated extraneous stories and added a number of transitions to make the story read more smoothly. Finally, she further researched the first Thanksgiving to finish her story with a flourish.

Alie's Final Storybook: "A Dream Come True," Alie's final book, is a wonderful artifact of her learning. Alie's oral history book had been delightful; however, the illustrations had been somewhat simplistic. Once she had finished with the

The voyage took 66 days. I sometimes got the scours from bad food and bad water. Then I would cast over the side. It was not a pleasant sight.

One year later we got married.

When I left, I hugged my mother and gave my sister my hat even though she was so small. I think she understood what was happening because she started to cry and when it was time to board I kissed my mother and sister. As the ship sailed away I watched the land fade away with my brave mother and my crying sister. I can still hear her crying over and over.

Sometimes I would love the peace and quiet in the meadows and the flowers that reminded me of Francis and mother. But one morn while I was in the meadows I saw a deer. Luckily I had my musket and I shot it and it brought it back and it was wonderful with stews water.

text of her oral history, Alie had raced through the drawings; she had needed the encouragement of her teachers and peers to make her drawings as good as the text. Her illustrations for her Pilgrim book were quite different. Inspired by the knowledge that I wanted to include her in my forthcoming book, Alie worked hard to create illustrations that did justice to her imaginative and lyrical text. Many of her classmates created elaborate borders for the text in their books, which inspired Alie to do so as well.

In her author's note, Alie wrote:

Most of my characters in my book are fictional, but John Billington. I also had to make my person as real as can be. It was hard because I am used to writing fiction. I wanted to make my person younger, but that didn't work out so I made him older. The reason he couldn't have come alone was he was too young. I also did a lot of research. I used *Mourt's Relation* a primary source that Pilgrims had written. I got my character's name from Edward Tilly with the made up last name, Milton, who comes from the real Mayflower [passenger] list.

Alie felt that she learned much more about the Pilgrims doing research this way instead of writing a conventional report: "It is more exciting." I believe she gained a remarkable amount of knowledge—about the process of research, the difference between fact and fiction, and a feel for what it means to learn about people of long ago.

A Wampanoag's Point of View

When planning the Pilgrim unit I had not intended to do anything formally with the Native American perspective. I was interested in having my students look deeply at the Pilgrim experience, to see if they could gain a feeling for what the Pilgrims' immigration to the New World was like and how it connected to the experience of immigrants today. However, as we got deeper into our study and as I did more research in preparation for our overnight trip to Plimoth Plantation, I decided that we did indeed need to look at the Wampanoag point of view.

Plimoth Plantation provides a great deal of material to help teachers prepare students for both points of view. A permanent exhibit called "Irreconcilable Differences: 1620 to 1692" presents both Pilgrim and Wampanoag perspectives on the events of the time. Next to the 1627 Pilgrim village is Hobbamock's Homesite. Hobbamock was a Wampanoag who, after the 1621 peace treaty with the Pilgrims, was sent to live near them in order to help them and function as an ambassador. The Plimoth Plantation site is a re-creation of his home, staffed by Native Americans who dress in traditional seventeenth-century clothing but who speak from a modern point of view. Thus, visitors can ask questions about both the seventeenth century and the Native Americans' lives today.

Shortly before our trip to Plimoth I began a mini-unit on the Wampanoag by reading aloud *Thunder from the Clear Sky* by Marcia Sewall. *Thunder from the Clear Sky* provides a compelling account of the distinctly different points of view that the Pilgrims and the Wampanoag had during the seventeenth century.

Next I divided the class into groups of four and gave each copies of essays written by Plimoth Plantation staff comparing Wampanoag and English lifestyles. The various essays were on family life, foodways, housing, furnishings, and clothing. Each began with a short introduction to the topic, contained sections describing Wampanoag and English conditions, and concluded with a list of sources. It was particularly important to me that my students be aware of the sources, something we had so emphasized during the storybook project.

Each group was to create a chart comparing the two groups on the subject of the essay they had read. Once they completed the charts they presented them to the class. This activity provided the children with an opportunity to use their newly acquired skills in reading for information (annotating, high-lighting, etc.) to gain a Wampanoag perspective.

My students easily understood that we weren't getting a totally fair per-spective. They recognized that much of the data on seventeenth-century Wampanoag life comes from the Pilgrims themselves, with all their potential for stereotyping. Since our main focus had been on the English settlers, how-ever, my students recognized that this was a mini-unit on the Wampanoag, intended to better prepare them for their trip to Plimoth Plantation, and that it was not a balanced view. To make it balanced would mean several more months of work—time we didn't have.

Lastly, I read Michael Dorris's *Guests* aloud. This is a moving book from a seventeenth-century Native American boy's perspective. His view of the strangers coming to his village for the harvest feast is not positive and provided my students with a different way of considering the Pilgrim experience. They were riveted during my reading, and when I was done I asked them what they thought.

"I used to think the Native Americans and Pilgrims really loved each other, and now I understand better how they were pretty uncomfortable with each other."

"Yeah, like the way the Indians think it is rude to look you in the eye while the Pilgrims would have thought it was rude not to."

"And all that stuff about having to feed the guests. What would happen next year?"

"It was cool seeing things from a different point of view."

Time Travel to Plimoth Plantation

On April 10 and 11, 1997, the Dalton fourth grade took their time travel trip to Plymouth, Massachusetts. Despite nervous parents ("Where is the nearest hospital?"), nervous children ("What if I hate all the food?"), nervous chaperones ("What about that five-hour bus trip?"), and a very nervous me ("What if they all hate it?"), everything worked out beautifully.

We left New York early and arrived at Plimoth Plantation in the early afternoon. After watching an orientation film together, we divided into small groups to tour the 1627 village. A sunny but cool day helped to make the experience a complete pleasure for all of us. We wandered about the village, seeking out people we knew of, such as William Bradford and Miles Standish. We watched a new house being built, enjoyed the animals, and were in awe of the small, rough houses. The interpreters were remarkably well prepared. Watching some women at the communal oven, Alie asked them who was the richest in the village. With Allerton as their answer, off we went for a visit. However, when Alie asked Mr. Allerton if he agreed that he was the richest, he laughed and said that it must have been his sister-in-law who had said so, and downplayed his own wealth. Excitedly, we sought out Governor Bradford and asked him about his first wife, who we knew had fallen overboard on the *Mayflower*. However, he refused to dwell on her, preferring to focus on his second wife and children. Charles suddenly remembered that he hadn't been able to find out Bradford's parents' names, so he asked the governor and was thrilled when Bradford obliged him with the information. Miles Standish, whom others in the village had warned us was a talker, did indeed bore us, going on and on about English history. I was amused by how shy many children became in the presence of the interpreters, and how I had to help them ask questions that would correlate with their knowledge. We also visited Hobbamock's Homesite. Many children especially enjoyed watching the Native Americans there create a canoe by burning the center of a log.

The special overnight program organized by the Plimoth Plantation staff included a colonial dinner, where the children had a grand time eating with their fingers while we adults enjoyed being served by our students, as would have happened in 1627. The food was very good, and many finicky eaters actually sampled some of it, grudgingly acknowledging that it was "okay." The evening continued with our playing colonial games, writing with a quill, and dressing up in Pilgrim clothes, and ended with the very tired time travelers sleeping soundly in the visitor's center.

The next morning, at the Pilgrim Hall Museum, we saw many Pilgrim artifacts, including Edward Winslow's portrait, William Bradford's chair, and the remains of the *Sparrowhawk,* a boat that was shipwrecked off the coast several years after the *Mayflower* journey. We also went aboard the *Mayflower II,* built in 1957 from meticulous research, and viewed Plymouth Rock, which my students knew was probably not the rock where the Pilgrims first stepped onto the New World, but rather a symbol of their importance in American history. After returning to the twentieth century with lunch at McDonald's, we boarded our buses and returned to New York City.

Reflecting Back

The Pilgrim unit gave me much to reflect on.

Dealing with Time

Teachers worry too much about time. I certainly did when planning this unit. I worried about how long it would take to teach the unit, how to get the children to understand just how long ago the Pilgrims lived, how far back in time to go. In retrospect, I think all that mattered was that the children understood that the Pilgrims lived a long time ago and that certain events happened before others. The mixed response to my Letters to the Future activity led me to wonder yet again where in children's development they refine their understanding of time to the point where an emphasis on teaching chronologically becomes necessary. My students understood that the Pilgrims lived a long time ago and that they were real people. Perhaps that is sufficient for fourth graders.

Valuing Historical Fiction

I love fantasy literature because it is so patently unreal. Historical fiction, however, has always bothered me because it is fiction presented as the real thing. When selecting books for the Pilgrim unit I avoided storybooks and historical fiction, seeking out books that seemed as factually accurate as possible. Thus, it was a complete surprise when I read Lasky's book, *A Journey to the New World,* and decided that it would be perfect for my class at that point in our study. The way this book helped my students imagine more clearly these people of the seventeenth century made me reconsider the value of historical fiction in the teaching of history. I am sure that I will actively seek out historical fiction for any future units that I develop.

Imaginary Characters versus Real People

When I came up with the idea of having my students use their immigrant oral histories as research models for their Pilgrim study I was certain that I wanted them to use an actual Pilgrim as a subject. We had a passenger list of the *Mayflower,* after all, and loads of information about them. It seemed to me that it would be easy to imagine these real people's answers to the oral history interview questions. However, I didn't anticipate my students' urge to be even more authentic than I had envisioned. They wanted specific information on these real people in order to answer the questions and did not wish to generalize from other sources. Their demand brought me up short and made me rethink how best to have children approach a project that involves real facts and imaginative thinking. The result is that I now recognize the value of composite characters based on real lives, the opposite of my original idea of using real people with made-up lives.

Balancing Process and Factual Knowledge

My students' self-evaluations at the end of the unit reinforced certain observations I had made during the project and surprised me as well. Activities that I had thought would be fun, such as the letters to the future, turned out to be meaningless for some children, while other activities that I thought would be hard and less fun turned out to be more meaningful to them. In reading over the self-evaluations it strikes me that the most successful experiences were those where the children were aware at the end of both the new factual knowledge and the process knowledge they had gained. I knew that they had learned a lot about reading for information, taking notes, and using factual information to create something new. They were able to better articulate that they had learned to read more challenging material and to write better, and had picked up a great deal of information about the Pilgrims. I suspect that as the process tools become embedded into their work as learners, it will be the facts of the Pilgrims that will consciously linger in their minds.

Imaginative Thinking

My students used their imaginations at every turn for this unit. We instinctively referred to our Pilgrim imaginary transcripts, spoke of how we pretended to be interviewing a Pilgrim, and constantly used the language of imagination in our conversations about these people of long ago. My students' knowledge about the Pilgrims and their enthusiasm for thinking about the past went far beyond what I had hoped for. I am now convinced more than ever of the importance of teachers' being conscious of the imagination when creating history curricula.

■ ■ ■

Our Pilgrim study had begun in the cold, dark days of January and ended in sunny April with our trip to Plimoth Plantation. While no mussels were consumed during our colonial overnight, the children did indeed feel as if they had traveled back in time. "I felt like I had really time warped," said Chris. "I saw people who dressed like Pilgrims, talked like Pilgrims, and even acted like Pilgrims. They cooked over a real fire and really planted crops and raised real animals. They erased all knowledge past 1627. Real proof of that was when Jesse showed them money the Pilgrim said he could write on it or throw it in the fire."

"I felt like an outcast from the future," said Alie.

And Bobby spoke for all when he said, "It felt good to go back in time."

 Zooming In

The Wampanoag

When studying the Pilgrims, it is important to include the experience of the Native American groups who lived in the area colonized by the Pilgrims. Students should come to understand the effects of colonization on existing indigenous populations. Even a brief examination of Native American culture will help provide a balanced and accurate picture of the historical period.

When the Pilgrims arrived at Plimoth, they came to a place that had been inhabited by native peoples for thousands of years. The Wampanoag were the Algonkian tribe who inhabited the area when the Pilgrims landed at Plimoth. The tribe numbered between 21,000 and 24,000, spread over southeastern Massachusetts, the coastal islands, and eastern Rhode Island. They had adapted to the environment in ways that ensured their survival for generations. They had grown accustomed to the seasonal cycles of abundance and scarcity in an environment they knew intimately. The Wampanoag combined farming, hunting and gathering, and fishing to achieve a diverse diet. Their staple crops were corn, beans, and squash. Other important crops included gourds, which they used as containers, and tobacco. Hunting for large and small game was most important when the harvest period was over. Families moved inland to hunt in small groups, returning to their traditional villages along the coast in time to plant again in the spring. Fishing was an important year-round activity, with inland streams and lakes supplementing the abundant supply of shellfish available from coastal waters year-round. Foraging for nuts, fruits, seeds, and berries was done by women and children according to their seasonal availability. The variety of foraged food supplemented the Wampanoag's diet throughout the year. Their varied use of resources allowed for seasonal cycles and enabled them to survive in the area for thousands of years.

The use of the environment by the European settlers differed radically from the way it had been used by Native American groups. By the end of the seventeenth century, the trade of natural resources for prestige goods, begun with the natives' first contact with Europeans, caused a profound transformation of the traditional ways of life of the indigenous people. Traditional life as known to the Wampanoag for generations was largely destroyed.

Although the Pilgrims observed Wampanoag practices, they had difficulty understanding various aspects of the organization of Wampanoag society. The division of labor between the sexes, the ease with which women could leave relationships with men who had treated them unfairly, the importance of reciprocity in terms of the redistribution of resources to ensure the survival of the group, Wampanoag religious practices, all were alien to the way of life the Pilgrims knew in Europe.

Although the Wampanoag leader Massasoit had signed a treaty with the Pilgrims as early as 1621, ensuring that the Wampanoag would not attack the Pilgrims and that the Pilgrims would back the Wampanoag in their struggles with other neighboring tribes, this did not guarantee peace for very long.

By the 1650s, conflicts over Wampanoag land being usurped by the influx of new settlers had escalated. Particularly difficult for the Wampanoag were the unfenced cattle that roamed through their farmland and destroyed their crops. By the late 1660s and 1670s hostilities between the Wampanoag and the Pilgrims had escalated, and both sides prepared for armed conflict. Led by Metacomet, known to the Pilgrims as King Philip, the Wampanoag and other tribes fought the colonists to protect their remaining land. The fighting that ensued during King Philip's War of 1675–1676 led to the end of Wampanoag control over their traditional land. Badly defeated, greatly reduced in numbers, and starving after much of their farmland was destroyed, the Wampanoag communities dispersed. Many of the Indians came under the control of Massachusetts colony once Plimoth was absorbed under its control. Other Indians were shipped to the West Indies or sold to colonists as indentured servants. Some were sent to reservations supervised by missionaries or the colonial government.

The legacy of the Pilgrims was devastating for the Wampanoag living on the mainland. While those Indians living on the islands off the coast managed to maintain their traditional life for almost another century, these communities also faced severe problems as colonization spread to their territories. By the end of the nineteenth century, the Wampanoag could no longer resist the domination of colonial power, and they controlled only a tiny fraction of their original territory. Their traditional way of life was largely destroyed.

The struggles of the Wampanoag continue, as they work collectively to revitalize their culture, strengthen the cultural identity of the youngest members of the tribe, and attain federal recognition and economic viability.

Students should learn about both the short-term and the long-term effects of the Pilgrim colony at Plimoth. By focusing only on the struggles and triumphs of the Pilgrims, it can be easy to overlook the devastating effects of colonization on the Wampanoag. Exploitation and decimation of indigenous peoples were part of the colonial period. Without presenting the experience of indigenous populations, stereotypes of an idyllic colonial past are perpetuated.

 Booktalk

Mourt's Relation: A Journal of the Pilgrims at Plymouth
edited by Dwight Heath

Mourt's Relation, first published in 1622 with the title *A Relation or Journal of the English Plantation settled at Plimoth,* is the earliest published account of the

Pilgrims' journey and experiences at Plimoth Plantation. It is a daily journal that describes everyday events and momentous occasions from November 1620 until December 1621, including the Pilgrims' exploration of Cape Cod, their first winter in the New World, and the first Thanksgiving. The book captures much of the spirit of adventure, from the attempts at mutiny on the ship to the Pilgrims' first encounters with the Wampanoag. The journal provides a wealth of information about the experiences of the settlers and their observations of the Wampanoag.

Authorship of the volume has been the subject of some debate. Attributed to several different authors, it is believed to have been written largely by Edward Winslow, with William Bradford also contributing major sections. According to editor Dwight Heath, Bradford's own volume, *Of Plymouth Plantation,* is almost identical to *Mourt's Relation* in its description of the first year at Plymouth. It is unclear who Mourt actually was; the name may be a pseudonym or a misprint of the name George Morton.

The volume is available in several formats. It can be read verbatim with its original headings, with only very minor spelling and punctuation changes. It is also available on-line, with substantial modifications that modernize the text. Whichever way you choose to use it, *Mourt's Relation* is an excellent source to read and use when studying the Pilgrims.

 ## Tools of the Trade

Using Primary Sources with Children

While using primary sources and documents is standard when teaching history in the upper grades, it seems a much more difficult option for middle school students. But just as students can be guided to use objects for learning history, so can they be helped to gain insights from primary sources. The critical issue is the selection of the appropriate sources—they must engage the students without being too difficult. A wide range of resources can be selected that go beyond the traditional documents used with older students. Letters and diaries, oral history transcripts, political pamphlets, and cartoons can all be introduced to young students as historical evidence to be analyzed. These sources can stimulate students' interest and help them formulate questions for further research.

Using a collection of primary sources, whether compiled for you or compiled by you, moves students closer to the way actual historians conduct research. Viewing a topic from different perspectives, sometimes looking at fragmentary evidence, students are able to construct their own interpretations in a way that textbooks don't usually encourage. Students have to weigh the validity of various accounts and attempt to explain some of the differences. Primary sources help students construct a more complete picture of the past. The challenge for teachers is to help students work with diverse materials and to find time to adequately evaluate primary sources of historical evidence.

Visiting Historic Sites

How far can you travel to create experiences for your students? While you may know about famous historic places, such as Williamsburg or Plimoth, are you aware of smaller historic sites, archaeological excavations, or re-creations that may be a shorter distance from your classroom? If your school will permit you to plan an overnight visit, expand your sights to places you can travel to in four or five hours. Through such sources as the National Register of Historic Places, the Association for Living Historical Farms and Agricultural Museums, and local historical societies you can find lists of locations in your area.

Historic places can evoke thoughts and feelings of time and place in a way that texts often cannot. In addition these sites present the physical manifestations of history in a way that is very different from museums. Visitors see authentic objects of everyday life in context, sometimes with actors in period costume telling stories from the past. When children get to use old tools, cook food, and participate in other activities of the period, they are likely to find the experience especially engaging. Historic places can provide an interesting way to evoke the past and enliven the study of history.

Researching On-Line

Several on-line resources can enhance a study of the Pilgrims. The pages mounted by Media 3 and maintained by Plimoth Plantation provide an excellent overview of the programs and the restoration there. The pages enable you to make a virtual tour of Plimoth Plantation by providing you with access to pictures of the re-creation of the settlement as it appeared in 1627 as well as pictures of Hobbamock's Homesite, the re-creation of a Wampanoag settlement. The Plimoth Plantation site also includes a library of essays on the Pilgrims and the Wampanoag, living histories and interpretations, recipes, annotated bibliographies, and color photographs of the restoration. Additional pictures of the plantation are contained within the University of Connecticut's Archnet Historical Database.

The most comprehensive Web site on the Pilgrims is Caleb Johnson's *Mayflower* Web pages. This site includes a vast number of resources on the *Mayflower,* including passenger lists, documents, the wills of *Mayflower* passengers, full texts of journals and books written by the Pilgrims, letters about the Pilgrims, and short essays on a variety of topics written by the author of the page, Caleb Johnson. The site also includes messages for both teachers and students about how to use the pages, as well as instructions for citations in research papers. It also provides links to other sites for genealogical research, an extensive bibliography, and a list of books available to purchase on-line.

For information on how to make use of historic places, visit the site maintained by the National Register of Historic Places. This site offers lesson plans, guides to developing your own lesson plans, and information about training workshops. The Web site mounted by the Association for Living Historical Farms and Agricultural Museums provides links to more than fifty international sites as well as an extensive bibliography and a glossary.

Here are the addresses of the sites mentioned above:

Plimoth Plantation: http://www.plimoth.org
Media 3 Plimoth site: http://media3.com/plimothplantation/vtour/
The Archnet Historical database:
    http://www.lib.uconn.edu/ArchNet/Topical/Historic/Plimoth
The *Mayflower* Web pages:
    http://member.aol.com/calebj/mayflower.html
National Register of Historic Places:
    http://www.cr.nps.gov/nr/twhp/home.html
Association for Living Historical Farms and Agricultural Museums Web site:
    http://www.mysticseaport.org/alhfam/
Association for Living Historical Farms and Agricultural Museums bibliography page:
    http://www.voicenet.com/~frstprsn/alhfam/lhbiblio.htm

Afterword

> The man shook his head. "No, no," he said. "I'm not being clear. It's not my past, not my childhood that I must transmit to you."
>
> He leaned back, resting his head against the back of the uphol-stered chair. "It's the memories of the whole world," he said with a sigh. "Before you, before me, before the previous Receiver and generations before him."
>
> Lois Lowry, *The Giver*

At first there seems to be no far away or long ago for Lois Lowry's dystopian community in her book *The Giver*. Twelve-year-old Jonas's knowledge of the past is limited to his own childhood recollections and the memories of those living around him. In this futuristic society, every-one is carefully cared for and distress and discomfort are seemingly avoided. Jonas, however, discovers a history before the living when he is selected to be the next Receiver of Memory. And as he receives memories good and bad, Jonas begins to view his community in a new light. Attitudes, routines, and behaviors that had seemed benevolent become reconfigured as cruel. Soon Jonas realizes that the community must take back its own history, painful as that might be.

Like Jonas's, our journey into history has been an illuminating one. We began with certain assumptions and had to alter them as we learned more, as we tried things out with children and then watched what happened, as we wrote and rewrote, and as we talked together and reflected on how to integrate our new knowledge into our old. With each unit, with each group of children, with each new piece of information, our own ideas of historical teaching and learning had to be reconfigured, including those concerning the following.

Time. Time continues to be important to us. How could it not be? History is about time, both the recent and the distant past. We continue to mull over how best to study time with children and how different people of different ages and cultures conceive of time in very different ways. For one fourth grader in April, the previous September can seem like a long time ago, while for another it is the seventeenth century that is a long time ago. Being open to different ways of considering the past is critical, we have found, to helping children construct their own notions of history.

Content. While we still are not prepared to state precisely what content should be taught and when, we are more convinced than ever that content does matter. We observed that rich content made history interesting and exciting for our students. At no point did any of them complain that history was boring. We believe the students enjoyed studying history because they found the subjects of the units interesting, the material compelling, and the topics ones they could make their own.

Sensitivity. Teachers can never be too sensitive when dealing with people's histories. Be it a child's family history or a community's history, it is critical to be always alert to the potential for offense. We found that as careful as we thought we were being, inadvertent slights and hurts still occurred. As teachers, we cannot know all the possible ways our work with history in the classroom may upset someone; however, always being aware of the need for sensitivity is a key concept we learned to keep in mind.

Imagination. Children's imagination is an untapped tool. Despite the common use of the word among educators, it seems to us that imagination has yet to be adequately utilized in children's learning, especially beyond the primary years. We hope to explore further the potential uses of students' imagination because we feel it has enormous possibilities in teaching and learning.

In *The Giver,* Jonas wonders at first why anyone should know about the past, but he begins to understand its importance as he receives memories from the old Receiver, now the Giver. With knowledge comes wisdom, and Jonas, with the Giver's help, constructs a new version of his community, one less kind but more truthful than his previous conception. Just as Jonas can be any and every one of our students seeking answers, so can the Giver be any of us teachers, providing the knowledge and help that allows each of our students, like Jonas, to forge a unique connection with the past.

Memories of the past, our own and others', is one way of defining history. Learning about these memories will always be useful. Which ones are important to know, how to bring them into the curriculum, and how to help children construct their own ideas of the past have been issues at the heart of this book. Teachers and students together must grapple with the complexities of knowledge every day. We hope that our society, unlike Jonas's, will continue to value knowledge of the past and keep struggling with the question of how best to give those memories to our custodians of the future.

References

Professional Books and Articles

Bigelow, Bill, Linda Christensen, Stan Karp, Barbara Miner, and Bob Peterson, eds. 1994. *Rethinking Our Classrooms: Teaching for Equity and Justice.* Milwaukee, WI: Rethinking Schools.

Brophy, Jere, and Bruce VanSledright. 1997. *Teaching and Learning History in Elementary Schools.* New York: Teachers College Press.

Brown, Cynthia Stokes. 1994. *Connecting with the Past: History Workshop in Middle and High Schools.* Portsmouth, NH: Heinemann.

Buerge, David, comp. 1992. *Chief Seattle.* Seattle: Sasquatch Books.

Burke, Peter, ed. 1992. *New Perspectives on Historical Writing.* University Park, PA: Pennsylvania State University Press.

Coles, Robert. 1989. *The Call of Stories: Stories and the Moral Imagination.* Boston: Houghton Mifflin.

Craik, F. I., and R. Lockhart. 1972. Levels of Processing: A Framework for Memory Research. *Journal of Verbal Learning and Verbal Behavior* 11: 671–684.

Downey, Matthew T., and Linda S. Levstik. 1991. Teaching and Learning History. In *Handbook of Research on Social Studies Teaching and Learning,* ed. James P. Shaver, 400–410. New York: Macmillan.

Dyson, Anne Haas, and Celia Genishi, eds. 1994. *The Need for Story: Cultural Diversity in the Classroom and Community.* Urbana, IL: National Council of Teachers of English.

Egan, Kieran. 1986. *Teaching as Storytelling: An Alternative Approach to Teaching and Curriculum in the Elementary School.* Chicago: University of Chicago Press.

———. 1992. *Imagination in Teaching and Learning: The Middle School Years.* Chicago: University of Chicago Press.

Facing the Storm. Editorial. *New York Times,* Jan. 9, 1996: 30.

Gardner, Howard. 1991. *The Unschooled Mind: How Children Think and How Schools Should Teach.* New York: Basic Books.

Grassian, Esther. 1995. Thinking Critically About World Wide Web Resources. UCLA College Library. http://www.library.ucla.edu/libraries/college/instruct/critical.htm.

Hirsch, E. D. 1996. *The Schools We Need and Why We Don't Have Them.* New York: Doubleday.

Holt, Tom. 1990. *Thinking Historically: Narrative, Imagination, and Understanding.* New York: College Examination Board.

Hubbard, Ruth Shagoury. 1996. *A Workshop of the Possible: Nurturing Children's Creative Development*. York, ME: Stenhouse.

Husbands, Chris. 1996. *What Is History Teaching? Language, Ideas, and Meaning in Learning About the Past*. Philadelphia: Open University Press.

Johnson, George. What Happens When the Brain Can't Remember. *New York Times,* July 7, 1996, section 4: 10.

Jorgensen, Karen. 1993. *History Workshop: Reconstructing the Past with Elementary Students*. Portsmouth, NH: Heinemann.

Kirby, Dan, and Carol Kuykendall. 1991. *Mind Matters: Teaching for Thinking*. Portsmouth, NH: Heinemann.

Kohl, Herbert. 1995. *Should We Burn Babar? Essays on Children's Literature and the Power of Stories*. New York: New Press.

Levstik, Linda S. 1997. Any History Is Someone's History: Listening to Multiple Voices from the Past. *Social History* 61, no. 1: 48–51.

Lowen, James W. 1995. *Lies My Teacher Told Me: Everything Your American History Textbook Got Wrong*. New York: New Press.

Nash, Gary B., and Charlotte Crabtree, co-directors. 1996. *National Standards for History*. Basic Edition. Los Angeles: University of California, National Center for History in the Schools.

Parkhurst, Helen. 1922. *Education on the Dalton Plan*. New York: Dutton.

Plimoth Plantation Staff. In press. *Field Book on Field Trips*. Plymouth, MA: Plimoth Plantation.

Quindlen, Anna. 1997. How Dark? How Stormy? I Can't Recall. *New York Times Book Review,* May 11, 1997: 35.

Rosenblatt, Louise. 1991. Literature—S.O.S. *Language Arts* 68, no. 6: 444–448.

Scott, Georgia. 1997. A Few Favorite Things: Treasured Mementos Hold Hope for Broken Lives. *New York Times,* March 30, 1997, section 13: 3.

Shuh, John H. 1982. Teaching Yourself to Teach with Objects. *Journal of Education* 7, no. 4: 8–15.

Sitton, Thad, George Mehaffy, and O. L. Davis, Jr. 1983. *Oral History: A Guide for Teachers (and Others)*. Austin: University of Texas Press.

Slapin, Beverly, and Doris Seale, eds. 1992. *Through Indian Eyes: The Native Experience in Books for Children*. Philadelphia: New Society Publishers.

Smith, Frank. 1990. *To Think*. New York: Teachers College Press.

Stott, John C. 1995. *Native Americans in Children's Literature*. Phoenix: Oryx Press.

Tally, Bill. History Goes Digital: Teaching When the Web Is in the Classroom. *D-Lib Magazine,* September 1996. http://www.dlib.org/dlib/september96/09tally.html. 15 July 1997.

Trachtenberg, Alan. 1989. *Reading American Photographs: Images as History, from Mathew Brady to Walker Evans*. New York: Hill and Wang.

Tunnell, Michael O., and Richard Ammon, eds. 1993. *The Story of Ourselves: Teaching History Through Children's Literature*. Portsmouth, NH: Heinemann.

Voris, Helen H., Maija Sedzielarz, and Carolyn P. Blackmon. 1986. *Teach the Mind, Touch the Spirit: A Guide to Focused Field Trips*. Chicago: Field Museum of Natural History.

Willis, Deborah, ed. 1994. *Picturing Us: African American Identity in Photography*. New York: New Press.

Zarnowski, Myra. 1990. *Learning About Biographies: A Reading and Writing Approach for Children*. Urbana, IL: National Council of Teachers of English; Washington, DC: National Council for the Social Studies.

———. 1995. Learning History with Informational Storybooks: A Social Studies Educator's Perspective. *The New Advocate* 8: 183–195.

Zinsser, William, ed. 1995. *Inventing the Truth: The Art and Craft of Memoir*. Boston: Houghton Mifflin.

Children's Books

Barry, Lynda. 1987. *In the Fun House*. New York: Harper and Row.

Baum, L. Frank. 1900. *The Wonderful Wizard of Oz*. Illus. W. W. Denslow. Chicago: George M. Hill Co.

Carroll, Lewis. 1966. *Alice's Adventures in Wonderland*. Illus. John Tenniel. London: Macmillan.

Cha, Dia. 1996. *Dia's Story Cloth*. Stitched by Chue and Nhia Thao Cha. New York: Lee & Low Books; Denver: Denver Museum of Natural History.

Cisneros, Sandra. 1984. *The House on Mango Street*. New York: Vintage Books.

Curtis, Christopher Paul. 1995. *The Watsons Go to Birmingham 1963*. New York: Delacorte Press.

Dahl, Roald. 1984. *Boy*. New York: Penguin.

Dorris, Michael. 1994. *Guests*. New York: Hyperion.

Eager, Edgar. 1956. *Knight's Castle*. Illus. N. M. Bodecker. New York: Harcourt Brace.

Fleichman, Sid. 1995. *The Thirteenth Floor: A Ghost Story*. Illus. Peter Sis. New York: Greenwillow Books.

Fritz, Jean. 1982. *Homesick: My Own Story*. New York: Dell.

Hoyt-Goldsmith, Diane. 1990. *Totem Pole*. Photos Lawrence Migdale. New York: Holiday House.

Jeffers, Susan. 1991. *Brother Eagle, Sister Sky*. New York: Dial Books.

King, Casey, and Linda Barrett Osborne. 1997. *Oh Freedom! Kids Talk About the Civil Rights Movement with the People Who Made It Happen*. New York: Knopf.

Knight, Margy Brun. 1993. *Who Belongs Here?* Illus. Anne Sibley O'Brien. Gardiner, ME: Tibury House.

Larson, Gary. 1989. *The PreHistory of the Far Side: A 10th Anniversary Exhibit*. Kansas City, MO: Andrews and McMeel.

Lasky, Kathryn. 1996. *A Journey to the New World: The Diary of Remember Patience Whipple*. New York: Scholastic.

Lawlor, Veronica, selector and illus. 1995. *I Was Dreaming to Come to America: Memories from the Ellis Island Oral History Project*. New York: Viking.

Lord, Bette Bao. 1984. *In the Year of the Boar and Jackie Robinson*. New York: HarperTrophy.

Lowry, Lois. 1993. *The Giver*. New York: Bantam Doubleday Dell.

Moss, Marissa. 1995. *Amelia's Notebook*. Berkeley, CA: Tricycle Press.

Peet, Bill. 1989. *An Autobiography*. Boston: Houghton Mifflin.

Rylant, Cynthia. 1982. *When I Was Young in the Mountains*. New York: Dutton.

Say, Allen. 1993. *Grandfather's Journey*. Boston: Houghton Mifflin.

Scieszka, Jon. 1995. *Math Curse*. Illus. Lane Smith. New York: Viking.

Speare, Elizabeth George. 1983. *Sign of the Beaver*. New York: Dell.

Stevenson, James. 1986. *When I Was Nine*. New York: Greenwillow Books.

Thurber, James. 1961. The Night the Bed Fell. In *My Life and Hard Times*. New York: Bantam.

Twain, Mark. 1917. *A Connecticut Yankee in King Arthur's Court*. New York: Harper.

White, E. B. 1952. *Charlotte's Web*. New York: Harper.

Zindel, Paul. 1993. *The Pigman and Me*. New York: Bantam.

Annotated Bibliographies

Memoirs

Fictionalized Memoirs

Barry, Lynda. 1988. *The Good Times Are Killing Me*. New York: HarperPerennial. Lynda Barry's weekly syndicated comic appears in a number of alternative newspapers. This novel is based on her life and was also performed as a play.

Cisneros, Sandra. 1984. *The House on Mango Street*. New York: Vintage Books. A series of brief but very moving chapters on a Latino family's life.

Curtis, Christopher Paul. 1995. *The Watsons Go to Birmingham 1963*. New York: Delacorte Press. A fictional account of an African American family in the 1960s.

Erlich, Amy, ed. 1996. *When I Was Your Age*. Cambridge, MA: Candlewick Press. A collection of original stories by well-known children's authors.

Nonfiction Memoirs

Byars, Betsy. 1991. *The Moon and I*. New York: Julian Messner. The popular author of the Bingo Brown books writes about herself as a writer.

Cleary, Beverly. 1988. *A Girl from Yamhill*. New York: Dell Yearling. Beverly Cleary's account of her early years. She has recently published a sequel to this book.

Dahl, Roald. 1984. *Boy*. New York: Penguin. The well-loved children's author writes about his childhood. *Going Solo,* the sequel, covers Dahl's young adulthood.

Foreman, Michael. 1989. *Warboy*. New York: Arcade. This English artist and children's book illustrator remembers his own childhood during World War II in this heavily illustrated volume. Recently, Foreman came out with a sequel, *After the War Was Over*.

Fritz, Jean. 1982. *Homesick: My Own Story*. New York: Dell. Fritz was born in China to American parents and lived there until she was twelve. This is a memoir of her time in China, of relations with Chinese friends, of a British school, and of feeling homesick for an America she had never seen.

Greenfield, Eloise, and Lessie Jones Little. 1979. *Childtimes*. New York: HarperTrophy. A lyrical memoir by three generations of a southern African American family.

Little, Jean. 1989. *Little by Little: A Writer's Education.* New York: Puffin Books. Little was born with very weak vision. This is her moving memoir of dealing with blindness and becoming a writer.

Mohr, Nicholasa. 1994. *Growing Up Inside the Sanctuary of My Imagination.* New York: Julian Messner. The author of *Felicida* tells her own story.

Naylor, Phyllis Reynolds. 1987. *How I Came to Be a Writer.* New York: Aladdin Books. Naylor, winner of the Newbery Award for *Shiloh,* tells her tale of becoming a writer.

Peet, Bill. 1989. *An Autobiography.* Boston: Houghton Mifflin. A charming, highly illustrated memoir by a veteran Disney animator.

Rylant, Cynthia. 1989. *But I'll Be Back Again.* New York: Orchard Books. The author of many beloved children's books, most recently *Dog Heaven,* writes of her own youth.

Singer, I. B. 1969. *A Day of Pleasure.* New York: Farrar, Straus and Giroux. The wonderful Yiddish writer tells of growing up in Warsaw.

Thurber, James. 1961. *My Life and Hard Times.* New York: Bantam. A collection of humorous essays about life with an extremely eccentric family.

Uchida, Yoshiko. 1991. *The Invisible Thread.* New York: Julian Messner. Memories of growing up Japanese-American in California and being interned in a camp during World War II.

Yep, Laurence. 1991. *The Lost Garden.* New York: Julian Messner. The author of *Dragonwings* tells of growing up on the West Coast in the 1950s.

Zindel, Paul. 1993. *The Pigman and Me.* New York: Bantam. The Pulitzer-Prize-winning author of *The Pigman* tells of his own crazy childhood on Staten Island.

Picture Books

Curtis, Jamie Lee. 1993. *When I Was Little: A Four-Year-Old's Memoir of Her Youth.* New York: HarperCollins. A sweet, amusing take on a child growing up little by little.

Ekoomiak, Normee. 1988. *Arctic Memories.* New York: Henry Holt. Beautiful illustrations by Ekoomiak coupled with descriptions give a firm sense of life in an Inuit home.

Garza, Carmen Lomas. 1990. *Family Pictures.* San Francisco: Children's Book Press. Beautiful illustrations of a particular Latino family's life.

Littlechild, George. 1993. *This Land Is My Land.* Emeryville, CA: Children's Book Press. Remarkable paintings captioned by Littlechild, based on his family memories.

Rylant, Cynthia. 1982. *When I Was Young in the Mountains.* New York: Dutton. A lyrical book based on Rylant's Appalachian background.

Stevenson, James. 1986. *When I Was Nine.* New York: Greenwillow Books. One of a series of books Stevenson has done on his childhood memories.

Cartoon Books

Barry, Lynda. 1987. *In the Fun House.* New York: Harper and Row. A collection of Lynda Barry's cartoons, clearly based on her memories. Many other collections are available.

Larson, Gary. 1989. *The PreHistory of the Far Side: A 10th Anniversary Exhibit.* Kansas City, MO: Andrews and McMeel. An imaginary exhibit presented as the Larson oeuvre from the beginning. Wonderful for lovers of cartoons.

Poetry

Hopkins, Lee Bennett. 1995. *Been to Yesterdays.* Honesdale, PA: Boyds Mills Press. A moving series of poems detailing Hopkins's difficult adolescence.

Reference

Menzel, Peter. 1994. *Material World: A Global Family Portrait.* San Francisco: Sierra Club Books. Large format photographic portrait of average families with their possessions capture elements of daily life in thirty countries.

Zinsser, William, ed. 1995. *Inventing the Truth: The Art and Craft of Memoir.* Boston: Houghton Mifflin. A fascinating series of interviews with well-known writers of memoirs. Parts are well worth reading aloud to children to inspire them.

Oral History

Books for Adults

Allen, Barbara, and Lynwood Montell. 1981. *From Memory to History: Using Oral Sources in Local Historical Research.* Nashville, TN: American Association for State and Local History. Guide to using oral history materials and techniques for evaluating available materials. Distributed by American Association for State and Local History, 172 Second Ave. N, Suite 102, Nashville, TN 37201.

Baum, Willa K. 1982. *Oral History for the Local Historical Society.* Nashville, TN: American Association for State and Local History. Written in a clear, accessible style by a leader in the development of oral history.

Dunaway, David K., and Willa K. Baum, eds. 1984. *Oral History: An Interdisciplinary Anthology.* Nashville, TN: American Association for State and Local History. Thirty-seven articles that discuss all aspects of oral history; includes many important pieces reprinted from other sources. Included in the anthology are articles by Alex Haley, Barbara Tuchman, and Allan Nevins.

Grele, Ronald J., et al. 1985. *Envelopes of Sound: The Art of Oral History.* 2nd ed. Chicago: Precedent Publishing. Essays based on a session on oral history held at a meeting of the Organization of American Historians in 1973, with selections added to reflect the changes that occurred in the field in the subsequent decade. Some of the essays are written as conversations and are meant to be read aloud.

Mehaffy, George L., Thad Sitton, and O. L. Davis, Jr. 1979. *Oral History in the Classroom: The How to Do It Series*. Washington, D.C.: National Council for the Social Studies. Short pamphlet, but provides a complete introduction to oral history projects. Available from NCSS Publications, 3501 Newark St. NW, P.O. Box P, Washington, D.C. 20016 (202-966-7840).

Sitton, Thad, George Mehaffy, and O. L. Davis, Jr. 1983. *Oral History: A Guide for Teachers (and Others)*. Austin: University of Texas Press. A thorough introduction to the techniques of oral history, including a discussion of project options, techniques, and equipment.

Terkel, Studs. 1995. *Coming of Age: The Story of a Century by Those Who Lived It*. New York: St. Martins Press. The most recent collection from the well-known and very popular oral historian, this volume traces the experiences of many individuals who contributed in various ways to the twentieth century. See also Terkel's other works, which include *American Dreams: Lost and Found* (New York: Ballantine Books, 1981); *The Good War: An Oral History of World War II* (New York: Ballantine Books, 1985); *Hard Times: An Oral History of the Great Depression* (New York: Pantheon, 1984); *Division Street: America* (New York: Pantheon, 1982); *Working: People Talk About What They Do All Day and How They Feel About It* (New York: Ballantine Books, 1985). Terkel is best known for including the voices of African American and working-class individuals in his histories.

Books for Children

Brown, Cynthia Stokes. 1988. *Like It Was: A Complete Guide to Writing Oral History*. New York: Teachers and Writers Collaborative. Excellent guide written by a distinguished teacher and author that takes students through the process of doing oral history. Includes a chapter on doing oral history in the classroom. Designed for ages twelve and up; useful for teachers as well.

Weitzman, David. 1975. *My Backyard History Book*. Boston: Little, Brown and Co. Provides project ideas for doing family and local history, written for elementary school children.

Wigginton, Eliot, ed. 1972–1986. *Foxfire 1–9*. New York: Doubleday. Series of books written by students who interviewed the elders of their community in Georgia.

Zimmerman, William. 1981. *How to Tape Instant Oral Biographies*. New York: Guarionex Press. Clear instructions for conducting oral history interviews, including questions to ask.

Northwest Coast Native Americans

Books for Adults

Bancroft-Hunt, Norman, and Werner Forman. 1988. *People of the Totem: The Indians of the Pacific Northwest.* Norman, OK: University of Oklahoma Press. An introduction to the peoples and cultures of the Northwest Coast, with many color photographs and illustrations of artifacts. Chapters on potlatch, the supernatural, myth and cosmology, dance, and ceremony.

Bruggmann, Maximilien, and Peter R. Gerber. 1989. *Indians of the Northwest Coast.* New York: Facts on File. Ethnologist Peter Gerber's text accompanies beautiful color photographs by Maximilien Bruggmann. Chapters on various groups and profiles of eleven contemporary artists make this a comprehensive reference tool.

Caraway, Caren. 1982. *Northwest Indian Designs.* Owings Mill, MD: Stemmer House Publishers. Black-and-white drawings of 49 designs from the textiles, metalwork, and ceramics of the native peoples of the Northwest Coast.

Cosgrove-Smith, Patricia. 1983. *Innovations for a Changing Time: Willie Seaweed: A Master Kwakiutl Artist.* Seattle: Pacific Science Center. Paperback catalog that accompanied an exhibit entitled "Smokey Top: The Art and Times of Willie Seaweed." The exhibit was unusual in its focus on a single artist. Although written for adults, the mixture of color photographs, historic photographs, and text make it an excellent introduction to the importance of seeing art as the work of particular individuals with particular histories.

Halpin, Marjorie. 1983. *Totem Poles: An Illustrated Guide.* Vancouver and Seattle: University of British Columbia Press and University of Washington Press. Describes the importance of totem poles on the Northwest Coast. Also suggests ways to interpret traditional and modern designs, and gives suggestions on how to look at poles. Although this is an adult book, the many black-and-white photographs and illustrations make this a useful reference for all ages.

Holm, Bill. 1965. *Northwest Coast Indian Art: An Analysis of Form.* Seattle: University of Washington Press. Most comprehensive discussion of graphic design in Northwest Coast art. Explains techniques and traditional patterns, as well as development of style and symbolism.

Jensen, Doreen, and Polly Sargent. 1986. *Robes of Power: Totem Poles on Cloth.* Museum Note No. 17. Vancouver: University of British Columbia Press. Catalog for the exhibit "Robes of Power." An excellent explanation of the importance of the button blanket, including interviews with elders, designers, and button blanket makers.

Jonaitis, Aldona, ed. 1991. *Chiefly Feasts: The Enduring Kwakiutl Potlatch.* New York: American Museum of Natural History with University of Washington Press. Catalog that accompanied an exhibition of the same name, with five essays that explain the history and meaning of the potlatch. Excellent photographs of objects as well as historic photographs, with informative captions.

Neel, David. 1992. *Our Chiefs and Elders: Words and Photographs of Native Leaders.* Vancouver and Seattle: University of British Columbia Press and University of Washington Press. Wonderful black-and-white portraits by a Kwakiutl photographer, showing the leaders in traditional dress as well as everyday clothing. Photographs are introduced with quotes drawn from Neel's conversations with the subjects.

Neel, David. 1995. *The Great Canoes: Reviving a Northwest Coast Tradition.* Vancouver and Seattle: Douglas and McIntyre and University of Washington Press. Color photographs and quotes from interviews with individuals from different Northwest Coast groups form the core of this book by Kwakiutl photographer David Neel. All aspects of canoe-building techniques are discussed, as well as the spiritual and ceremonial importance of canoes. Neel sees the building of canoes as a metaphor for community. Also includes ten rules of canoe building developed by the Quileute canoe contingent, a Northwest experiential education conference held in 1990. An eloquent book.

Steltzer, Ulli. 1984. *A Haida Potlatch.* Seattle: University of Washington Press. A photographic record of a potlatch held in 1981, with quotes from potlatch speeches and interviews. Black-and-white photographs capture the emotions as well as record the events. Introduction provides background information about potlatch.

Stewart, Hilary. 1984. *Cedar: Tree of Life to the Northwest Coast Indians.* Seattle: University of Washington Press. Comprehensive reference with excellent descriptions and drawings of every aspect of the use and importance of cedar.

Time-Life Books. 1993. *Keepers of the Totem.* Alexandria, VA: Time-Life Books. A thorough discussion of both traditional and modern practices of Northwest Coast groups. Chapters describe different kinds of potlatches, the carving of a canoe, and a totem pole raising in 1991. Includes wonderful color photographs of modern potlatches and canoe carving as well as historic photographs.

Books for Children

Adams, Dawn. 1985. *Potlatch.* Vancouver: WEDGE, The University of British Columbia. One of a series of readers written for the Queen Charlotte Islands Schools to provide children with reading materials based on their own cultural practices. Although the suggested age range is 5–12 years, the reading level is listed as being for beginning second graders. Illustrated with drawings based on photographs taken by the author, the book would be of interest to older children in the context of learning about books written specifically for Native American children.

Beyer, Don E. 1991. *The Totem Pole Indians of the Northwest.* New York: Franklin Watts. General introduction to life on the Northwest Coast, with color illustrations of artifacts and a few historic photographs. Very little on contemporary life.

Bonvillain, Nancy. 1994. *The Haidas.* Brookfield, CT: Millbrook Press. One of a series of books on Native Americans, well written with beautiful color illustrations. Includes information about traditional practices and values as well as contemporary life.

Cohlene, Terri, and Charles Reasoner. 1990. *Clamshell Boy: A Makah Legend.* Vero Beach, FL: Watermill Press. Illustrated telling of a Makah myth, with drawings and photographs. Concluding chapter has information about historical and contemporary life; book includes a time line and a glossary.

Jensen, Vickie. 1994. *Carving a Totem Pole.* New York: Henry Holt. A look at how a totem pole is carved, showing that poles tell stories and are an important linkage to the past. Striking black-and-white photographs taken by the author accompany an excellent text.

McDermott, Gerald. 1993. *Raven.* San Diego: Harcourt Brace Jovanovitch. Retelling of one of the myths of Raven with color illustrations.

McNutt, Nan. 1984. *The Bentwood Activity Book.* Petersburg, AK: Workshop. A book that provides directions for making a box out of cardboard, based on the techniques for making bentwood boxes. Very clear directions, with explanatory text as well. (Available from Nan McNutt, Box 295, Petersburg, AK 99833.)

McNutt, Nan. 1986. *The Button Blanket Activity Book.* Petersburg, AK: Workshop. (Available from Nan McNutt, Box 295, Petersburg, AK 99833.) How to make a button blanket, with concise instructions and good illustrations.

McNutt, Nan. 1991. *The Cedar Plank Book: An Activity Book for Ages 9–12.* Petersburg, AK: Workshop. (Available from Nan McNutt, Box 295, Petersburg, AK 99833.) In addition to instructions for mask-making and other activities, the book presents a story of a Nuu-chah-nulth (Makah) boy and his grandfather and a family mask the boy will inherit.

Murphy, Claire Rudolf, and Duane Pasco. 1993. *The Prince and the Salmon People.* New York: Rizzoli. Based on anthropologist Franz Boas's material and interviews with Tsimshian elders and artisans. The story of a young prince's journey to an underwater world where he meets the chief of the Salmon People, who is his uncle. Illustrated by Tsimshian artist Duane Pasco; also includes color photographs of art from museum collections.

Porter, Frank W. 1989. *The Coast Salish Peoples.* New York: Chelsea House. This volume focuses on the political struggles of the groups who live around Puget Sound in Washington state to gain historic and contemporary title to their land. Written for older students.

Shemie, Bonnie. 1992. *Houses of Wood.* Plattsburg, NY: Tundra Books. Straightforward discussion of three major house types in the Pacific Northwest. Book takes readers through the stages of house construction from felling the trees to completion, including a section on life in the house.

Walens, Stanley. 1992. *The Kwakiutl.* New York: Chelsea House Publishers. Written for older students, this book is an excellent overview on Kwakiutl traditional culture, with chapters devoted to the gold rush and to the potlatch. Also includes a discussion of contemporary issues and cultural revitalization programs.

Magazine Articles

Freed, Stanley. 1985. "Potlatch: An Indian Ceremony." *Faces Magazine: All Kinds of Gifts* 2, no. 3 (December). Introduction to the potlatch, written by the Curator of North American Indians at the American Museum of Natural History.

Kvietock, Peter. 1986. "Totem: Images of Family History." *Faces Magazine: Animal Allies* 2, no. 8 (May). Short article on totems written by the Assistant Registrar at the American Museum of Natural History.

Videos

The Box of Daylight: A Tlingit Myth of Creation. 1990. Juneau, AK: Pacific Communications and Marketing. Running time: 8.5 minutes.

In the Land of the War Canoes: A Drama of Kwakiutl Life in the Northwest. 1914. New York: Milestone Film and Video. Running time: 47 minutes.

Pilgrims

Books for Adults

Bradford, William. 1981. *Of Plymouth Plantation, 1620–1647.* S. E. Morison, ed. Introduction by Francis Murphy. New York: Modern Library. This highly readable account, written by the second governor of Plimoth, documents life in that settlement between 1620 and 1647.

Briggs, Helen, and Rose Briggs. 1990. *Picture Guide to Historic Plymouth.* Revised by Hope A. Thurlby. Plymouth, MA: Pilgrim Society. Brochure containing black-and-white photographs of sites in historic Plymouth with descriptions of each site. Useful if planning a trip to Plimoth Plantation and looking for other sites to visit.

Heath, Dwight, ed. 1963. *Mourt's Relation: A Journal of the Pilgrims at Plymouth.* Bedford, MA: Applewood Books. A reprint of the first account of the Pilgrims at Plimoth Plantation and their emigration. Published originally in England in 1622.

Josslyn, John. [1672.] *New England Rarities Discovered.* Old Saybrook, CT: Applewood Press. This reprint of a 1672 document identifies plants and animals of New England, as well as the medicinal uses of plants.

Winslow, Edward. [1624.] *Good Newes from New England: A True Relation of Things Very Remarkable at the Plantation of Plimoth in New England.* Bedford, MA: Applewood Books. Reprint of a document first published in 1624, which was instrumental in persuading English citizens to come to Plimoth. With annotations from 1841, the book contains information about the land and native peoples who had inhabited New England before the arrival of the Pilgrims.

Books for Children

Brown, Margaret Wise, ed. 1988. *Homes in the Wilderness: A Pilgrim's Journal of Plymouth Plantation in 1620, by William Bradford and Others of the Mayflower Company.* Hamden, CT: Linnet Books. A reprint of the original (1939) edition, a modern translation and adaptation of *A Relation or Journal of the Proceedings of the Plantation Settled at Plymouth in New England,* better known as *Mourt's Relation.* Illustrated with black-and-white drawings by Mary Wilson Stewart.

Glubok, Shirley. 1970. *The Art of Colonial America.* New York: Macmillan. Survey of colonial art, artifacts, and architecture with black-and-white photographs.

Penner, Lucille Recht. 1991. *Eating the Plates: A Pilgrim Book of Food and Manners.* New York: Scholastic. A discussion of the eating habits, customs, and manners of the Pilgrims in accessible prose, with black-and-white photographs and illustrations. Includes recipes for preparing a Pilgrim meal.

Roop, Connie, and Peter Roop, eds. 1995. *Pilgrim Voices: Our First Year in the New World.* New York: Walker and Co. An adaptation of *Mourt's Relation* and *Of Plimoth Plantation,* using modern language to tell the story of the first year at Plimoth.

Sans Souci, Robert. 1991. *N. C. Wyeth's Pilgrims.* Paintings by N. C. Wyeth. San Francisco: Chronicle Books. The author's text accompanies N. C. Wyeth's paintings of Plimoth, fourteen murals that present a somewhat romanticized version of Pilgrim life.

Sewall, Marcia. 1986. *The Pilgrims of Plimoth.* New York: Atheneum. The daily life of the Pilgrims at Plimoth told with text and paintings by the author. Includes a glossary of unfamiliar terms.

Sewall, Marcia. 1995. *Thunder from the Clear Sky.* New York: Atheneum. Companion volume to *The Pilgrims of Plimoth,* this book focuses on the encounters between the Wampanoag and the Pilgrims using parallel, alternating story lines and evocative paintings by the author.

Stein, R. Conrad. 1995. *The Pilgrims.* Chicago: Children's Press. The story of the Pilgrims' journey and their first few years in Plymouth Colony, with a brief discussion of the place of the settlement in American history. Includes a glossary and a time line.

Travers, Carolyn Freeman, ed. 1989. *Plimoth Plantation: A Pictorial Guide*. Plymouth, MA: Plimoth Plantation. A well-photographed pamphlet that describes the journey, the Plantation, Hobbamock's Wampanoag Indian homesite, the *Mayflower II,* and the concept of living history. It also provides a behind-the-scenes look at Plimoth Plantation.

Waters, Kate. 1989. *Sarah Morton's Day: A Day in the Life of a Pilgrim Girl.* Photos by Russ Kendall. New York: Scholastic. Excellent color photographs taken at Plimoth Plantation enliven this portrait of a day in the life of a young girl at Plimoth. The book identifies Sarah as a real person and also provides information about the child who portrays her at Plimoth.

Waters, Kate. 1993. *Samuel Eaton's Day: A Day in the Life of a Pilgrim Boy.* Photos by Russ Kendall. New York: Scholastic. Second in a series of re-creations of life at Plimoth, this book focuses on the life of a young boy who arrived in Plimoth in 1627. The child who portrays Samuel is a descendant of an original settler, and his family still lives in Plimoth.

Waters, Kate. 1996. *On the Mayflower: Voyage of the Ship's Apprentice and a Passenger Girl.* Photos by Russ Kendall. New York: Scholastic. Story about the interaction between a fictional *Mayflower* apprentice and a real passenger, with excellent color photographs taken on the *Mayflower II,* a reproduction of the original *Mayflower.*

Waters, Kate. 1996. *Tapenum's Day: A Wampanoag Indian Boy in Pilgrim Times.* Photos by Russ Kendall. New York: Scholastic. Third in a series of re-creations of life in the 1620s, this book focuses on the Wampanoag, the native people who lived in the Plimoth region. The book documents life at Hobbamock's Homesite at Plimoth Plantation. In contrast to the life of the Pilgrims portrayed at Plimoth, the people working at the Wampanoag homesite do not pretend to be actual characters from 1620, and they talk to visitors from a modern perspective.

Ziner, Feenie. 1961. *The Pilgrims and Plymouth Colony.* New York: American Heritage Co. An older text with color illustrations, written for older children.

Informational Storybooks

Bowen, Gary. 1994. *Stranded at Plimoth Plantation,* 1626. New York: HarperCollins. Beautifully illustrated with woodcuts, this book is based on historical accounts and documents from 1626 and 1627. It tells the story of a thirteen-year-old orphan who was stranded at Plimoth until it could be arranged for him to go Jamestown, and who lived with a family that had arrived at Plimoth six years before.

Dalgliesh, Alice. 1954. *The Thanksgiving Story.* New York: Charles Scribner's and Sons. Simple picture book story of one family's first Thanksgiving, with illustrations by Helen Sewell.

Harness, Cheryl. 1995. *Three Young Pilgrims*. New York: Aladdin Paperbacks. An illustrated storybook that blends fact with fiction.

Lasky, Kathryn. 1996. *A Journey to the New World—The Diary of Remember Patience Whipple*. New York: Scholastic. A fictional account of the life of a young girl at Plimoth.

Van Leeuwen, Jean. 1995. *Across the Wide Dark Sea: The Mayflower Journey*. New York: Dial Books for Young Readers. The story of a boy and his family, their journey on the *Mayflower*, and their experiences during the first winter at Plimoth Plantation.

Index

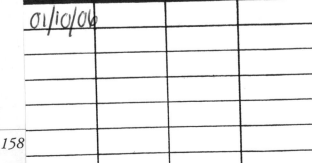

DATE DUE

01/10/06			